I0434880

2011 Science Accomplishments

 USDA PACIFIC NORTHWEST RESEARCH STATION

Vision and Mission

We are highly sought for our scientific leadership and impartial knowledge. Our mission is to generate and communicate scientific knowledge that helps people understand and make informed choices about people, natural resources, and the environment.

Moose Pass, Chugach Range, south-central Alaska. Photo by Jon Williams.

Contents

A Message From the Station Director

EXPERTISE, dedication, and partnership: these are key elements to success within the Pacific Northwest Research Station. Fostering these elements enables the station to generate timely scientific information for land managers and policymakers to use for decisions about managing natural resources.

In 2011, several projects examined ecosystem processes across large landscapes. The Integrated Landscape Assessment Project, for example, developed models for assessing wildlife habitat, fire risk, vegetation, development, and likely effects of climate change across watersheds in Washington, Oregon, Arizona, and New Mexico. These models are helping public and private land managers prioritize management efforts.

Bov B. Eav

Another project examined changes in old forests in the 15 years since the Northwest Forest Plan went into effect. Byproducts of this effort have given forest managers rare, seamless information that spans ownerships, allowing owners to consider how their management decisions fit into the broader landscape.

As we tackle questions at large scales of analysis, our partnerships with other agencies, nongovernmental organizations, tribes, and universities grow in importance. Together we leverage our expertise to address relevant questions, provide information to long-time stakeholders, and become acquainted with new stakeholders.

This year we made significant progress toward improving the physical spaces that will enable research and partnerships to flourish. In Oregon, construction is well underway on the new wing of the Corvallis Forestry Sciences Laboratory located on the Oregon State University campus. This energy-efficient building will provide shared laboratory and office space for scientists and support staff from the station, the Siuslaw National Forest, and the Natural Resource Information System group.

Construction began in August on the new Juneau Forestry Science Laboratory on land adjacent to the University of Alaska Southeast. Like the Corvallis Laboratory, this facility is being constructed to meet or exceed the Leadership in Energy and Environment silver certificate requirements. The energy efficiencies will mean lower energy costs and a smaller carbon footprint.

Proximity to the campus, which is also home of the station-sponsored Alaska Coastal Rainforest Center, will facilitate collaborative research.

The station remains a key supporter of the Alaska Coastal Rainforest Center, which was started in 2009 as a collaborative effort to expand and enhance education and research opportunities among six partners. It now has 14 partners, including the Tlingit and Haida Indian Tribes of Alaska, the City of Juneau, British Columbia Ministry of Forestry, U.S. federal agencies, and nongovernmental organizations. The center is becoming a research hub; in 2012 it will host the international symposium "Coastal Temperate Rainforests: Integrating Communities, Climate Science, and Resource Management."

The station continues to improve its service to underserved communities. Station scientists worked with the Muckleshoot Indian Tribe in Washington state to develop new elk habitat models. Elk are an important cultural resource for the tribe. Scientists and partners are also mapping public land use by the Hispanic community in Washington. This project arose after a Hispanic man harvesting floral greens in a forest was accidentally shot by a hunter. The maps will be used to generate dialog with state and federal agencies about harvester safety.

In 2012, new projects will include a study of the forest dynamics after thinning and fuel reduction at Pringle Falls Experimental Forest. This experiment has been designed to test which fuel treatments best accelerate development of large trees while reintroducing natural disturbance processes that provide ecosystem resilience. Another question considers the interactions between climate change and fuel treatments on vegetation dynamics and forest structure. These are timely questions—answers to which will surely provide insight to management issues across dry forests of the West.

Thank you to station partners and employees for a productive year, and I look forward to our work together in 2012.

Station Director Bov B. Eav

Pacific Northwest Research Station: The Setting

▸ The Pacific Northwest Research Station is one of five research stations in the U.S. Department of Agriculture, Forest Service

▸ Headquarters are in Portland, Oregon

▸ 11 laboratories and centers in Alaska, Oregon, and Washington

▸ 12 active experimental areas (forests, ranges, and watersheds)

▸ Research is conducted in more than 20 research natural areas

▸ 413 employees (311 permanent, 102 temporary)

Jon Williams

Southeast Alaska

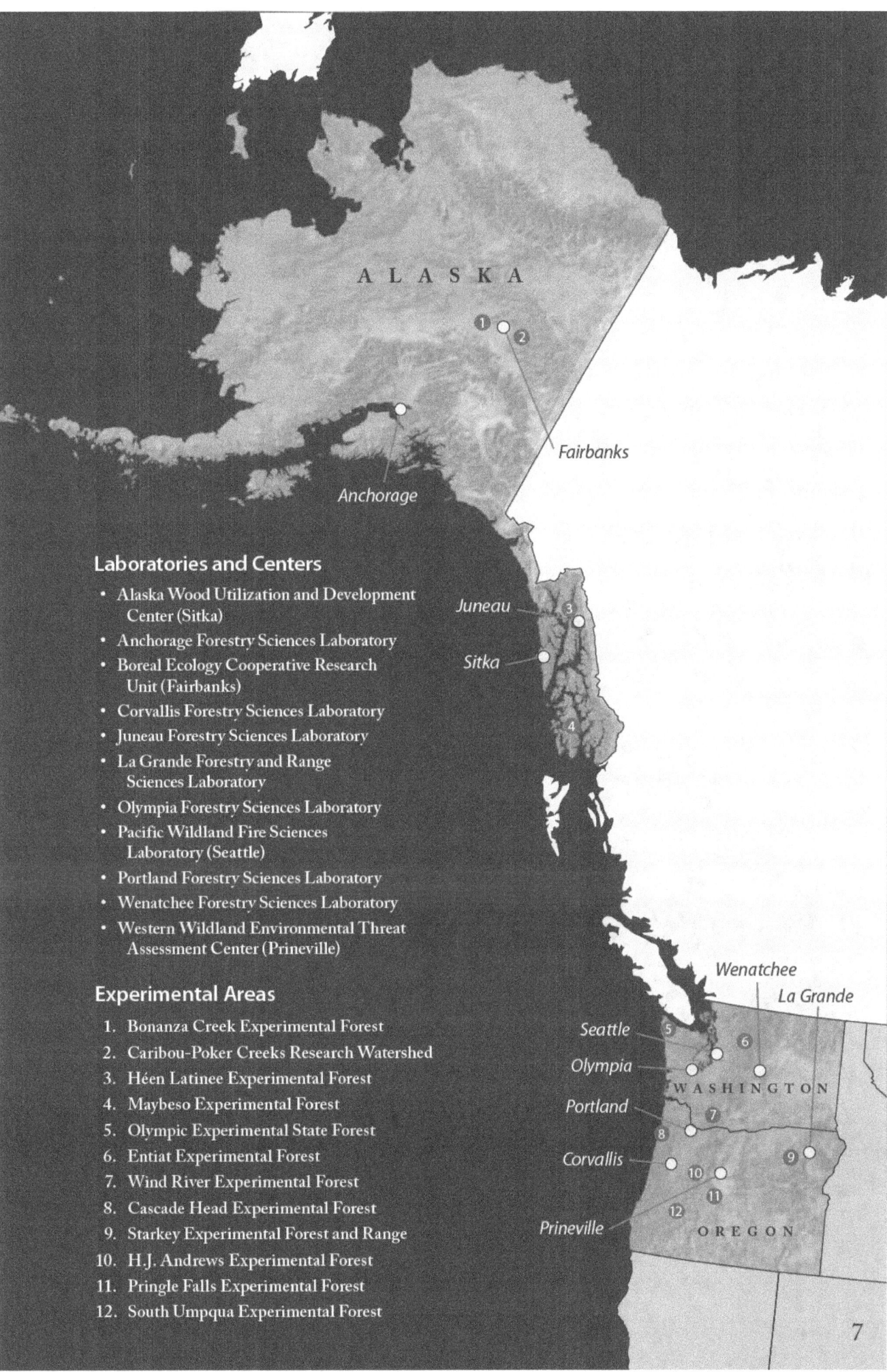

A L A S K A

1
2

Fairbanks

Anchorage

Laboratories and Centers

- Alaska Wood Utilization and Development Center (Sitka)
- Anchorage Forestry Sciences Laboratory
- Boreal Ecology Cooperative Research Unit (Fairbanks)
- Corvallis Forestry Sciences Laboratory
- Juneau Forestry Sciences Laboratory
- La Grande Forestry and Range Sciences Laboratory
- Olympia Forestry Sciences Laboratory
- Pacific Wildland Fire Sciences Laboratory (Seattle)
- Portland Forestry Sciences Laboratory
- Wenatchee Forestry Sciences Laboratory
- Western Wildland Environmental Threat Assessment Center (Prineville)

Experimental Areas

1. Bonanza Creek Experimental Forest
2. Caribou-Poker Creeks Research Watershed
3. Héen Latinee Experimental Forest
4. Maybeso Experimental Forest
5. Olympic Experimental State Forest
6. Entiat Experimental Forest
7. Wind River Experimental Forest
8. Cascade Head Experimental Forest
9. Starkey Experimental Forest and Range
10. H.J. Andrews Experimental Forest
11. Pringle Falls Experimental Forest
12. South Umpqua Experimental Forest

Juneau

Sitka

3

4

Wenatchee

La Grande

Seattle   5

Olympia   6

Portland

Corvallis   7

Prineville   8

W A S H I N G T O N

9

10

11

12

O R E G O N

Highlights From 2011

THE PACIFIC NORTHWEST (PNW) Research Station conducts research on a wide range of topics to improve the management and use of natural resources. Categorizing this research is often difficult because in many cases the crux of an issue lies in its connection to many natural processes. Climate change, for example, affects all natural processes and thus is an inherent component of much of the station's research. The following section highlights emerging narratives from research described in more detail throughout the report.

Living With a Changing Climate

Providing information to help land managers and decisionmakers plan for a changing climate

THE EFFECTS of warmer global temperatures are far reaching, yet nuanced: local effects will differ. Station scientists are studying climate change from many angles. Their work is instrumental in providing land managers and policymakers with needed tools and information to manage the Nation's natural resources under changing conditions.

Managing for Change

The North Cascadia Adaptation Project—This collaborative effort was developed by the Forest Service and the National Park Service with a goal of incorporating climate change adaptation into current management on federal lands in northern Washington.

▷ **A vulnerability assessment and climate change adaptation strategy** for Olympic National Forest and Olympic National Park (**http://www.treesearch.fs.fed.us/pubs/38702**).

▷ **Education workshops** for 330 staff from the Mount Baker-Snoqualmie National Forest, Okanogan-Wenatchee National Forest, Mount Rainier National Park, and North Cascades National Park.

American Indian and Alaska Native Tribes—They face disproportionate risks associated with climate change because of their close cultural and economic relationship to the land. A station scientist and university partners develop collaborative tools to help build awareness of the unique problems faced by tribal stakeholders and document tribes' innovative approaches to adaptation.

▷ The Lummi Nation and Swinomish, Coquille, and Nez Perce Tribes used the collaborative model to initiate climate adaptation planning.

▷ The collaborative model was replicated in Forest Service Research and Development (R&D) across the agency as part of the All Station Tribal Climate Change Initiative.

Assisted Adaptation

Understanding the role of genetics in the adaptive ability of plants. This is important so that seed sources can be matched with planting locations.

▷ **Seed transfer zones developed for mountain brome**, a grass commonly used in restoration efforts and used by the Malheur, Ochoco, Umatilla, and Wallowa-Whitman National Forests.

▷ **More than 38,000 genes identified** in Douglas-fir and 21,000 genes in two subspecies of big sagebrush.

Richard C. Johnson

Researchers developed seed transfer zones for mountain brome.

Change in the Far North

Understanding carbon loss—The largest fire ever recorded on the Arctic slope, in 2007, led to new knowledge of carbon levels in Alaskan tundra.

▷ Carbon released to the atmosphere by the 600-square-mile fire was 20 times more carbon than what is annually lost from undisturbed tundra, according to estimates by station scientists and collaborators.

▷ Techniques were implemented that measure carbon loss in tundra areas. Tundra permafrost stores carbon sequestered for millennia. Frequent wildfires could release this carbon, leading to further global warming.

◁ Under a formal work agreement with the U.S. Geological Survey, a station scientist helped develop models to forecast the future viability of polar bears under different climate scenarios. The polar bears were safely anesthetized and subsequently released unharmed. Photo by Steve Amstrup.

American Recovery and Reinvestment Act

Creating new jobs while promoting healthy ecosystems

THE PNW Research Station directed $14.2 million under the 2009 American Recovery and Reinvestment Act (ARRA) toward projects addressing fuel treatments, smoke impacts, salmon habitat, and natural systems in urban areas.

▷ More than 220 people, with skills ranging from construction to field data collection to high-tech computer modeling, have been employed for varied lengths of time.

▷ Students at the University of Oregon School of Journalism and Communications are helping tell the economic recovery story. Multimedia packages developed by the students are at http://sciencestories.uoregon.edu/.

Dede Olson

An Oregon State University employee hired with American Recovery and Reinvestment Act (ARRA) funds directed through the station explains an ARRA project to University of Oregon journalism students.

Completed projects

New Solar-Powered Stream Gauge Stations

▷ At South Umpqua Experimental Forest, dilapidated, unsafe stream gauge stations were replaced by new solar-powered facilities on Coyote Creek (known for its high-quality salmon habitat).

Jobs: 10

Olympia Lab Windows Replacement

▷ Single-pane windows from the 1960s were replaced with modern energy-efficient windows to retain heat in the winter and keep the building cool in the summer.

Jobs: 10

Road Maintenance

▷ Infrastructure and erosion control improvement projects were completed, including bridge replacement, resurfacing roads, and correcting drainage issues.

Jobs: 20

Impact of Economic Recovery Funding in Rural Communities

Roadside brush removal being conducted by hand crews on the Six Rivers National Forest.

▷ Social and economic impacts of ARRA-funded projects were evaluated in eight economically distressed rural areas across the United States. Forest Service investments in projects helped meet the goals of the Recovery Act, with investments having far-reaching social and economic benefits for rural communities.

Jobs: 12

Projects in progress

Smoke Forecasting

Outcomes   ▷ Reduce human health hazards by providing timely smoke forecasting.

▷ Deliver accurate smoke forecasts from both wild and prescribed fires.

▷ Accelerate development of improved tools for smoke and fire management.

Jobs: 20. To continue through 2012.

Restoring Critical Habitat for Listed Pacific Salmon

Outcomes   ▷ Assess watersheds in southeast Alaska and the interior Columbia Basin vulnerable to climate change.

▷ Identify key places for habitat restoration.

▷ Examine climate change and fire effects on watershed and fish habitat.

▷ Map fish habitat in southwest Oregon and northwest California.

▷ Develop a stream chemistry tool for establishing water-quality regulations for timber harvest.

Jobs: 20. To continue through 2012.

◁ Earth Corps volunteers help stabilize a shoreline in the Seattle metropolitan area. Station scientists and cooperators are studying what motivates people to engage in urban stewardship activities to make the most of citizen involvement efforts. Photo by Earth Corps.

Adapting Forests to Climate Change Effects

Outcomes
▷ Assess contribution of urban trees to carbon sequestration, energy savings, water management, and quality of life for residents.

▷ Provide baseline data on forest conditions in populated areas in five western states.

Jobs: 15 to date. To continue through 2013.

Contractors receive training from station specialists about how to inventory urban forests in Portland, Oregon.

Youth Summer Employment and Education

Outcomes
▷ Provide leadership and learning opportunities in natural resources for students in middle school to graduate school.

▷ Hire college interns to collect data on the timing of bud burst, bud set, and growth periods of Douglas-fir, toward developing seed transfer zones.

▷ Hire and train high-school and college students to collect data on riparian vegetation, soil, and habitat quality at sites in the Portland-Vancouver metropolitan area in a study of the response of riparian areas to urbanization.

Jobs: 13 to date. To continue through 2012.

Integrated Landscape Assessment

Outcomes
- ▷ Help prioritize land management at the watershed scale in Arizona, New Mexico, Oregon, and Washington.
- ▷ Assess wildlife habitat, community economics, fire risk, vegetation development, and likely effects of climate change.
- ▷ Provide webinars on fuels characteristics, decision support, climate change, and vegetation. Presentations are available at http://oregonstate.edu/inr/ilap-webinars.

Jobs: 60. To continue through 2013.

Station scientists and partners in Arizona's Sky Islands. Tools and information from the Integrated Landscape Assessment Project can be used in watershed restoration strategies, forest plan revisions, statewide assessments, and bioregional plans.

Ecosystem Restoration in the Puget Sound Area

Outcome
- ▷ Provide municipalities with information to plan for green spaces and development in urbanizing areas through ecosystem restoration.

Jobs: 30. To continue through 2013.

Fuel Loads and Tree Mortality

Outcome
- ▷ Field-test new technology to reduce tree mortality from bark beetles and sudden oak death, toward lessening risk of uncontrollable wildfire and impacts on nearby communities.

Jobs: 2. To continue through 2013.

◁ An intern hired with ARRA funds records weather data for a project that will develop seed transfer zones for Douglas-fir. Photo by Connie Harrington.

Assessing Threats to Shrub-Steppe Ecosystems

Station scientists are working with partners to conserve the wildlife and plants in this unique landscape

DUSKY SAGEBRUSH spreading across an expansive landscape: an iconic scene of the American West. It's also one of the most threatened ecosystems in the country. Invasive cheatgrass, changing fire regimes, encroaching juniper trees, and human development are taking a toll on shrub-steppe ecosystems.

Cheatgrass and juniper invasions

Cheatgrass, a nonnative, highly flammable grass, is altering historical fire cycles in sagebrush shrublands. Intense fires favor the invasive grass and threaten the survival of sagebrush and other native vegetation. Encroaching juniper can exacerbate soil erosion, reduce forage, and highten risk of crown fires.

▷ Expected spread of cheatgrass and juniper was mapped in the Columbia Basin.

▷ Models were developed to predict the risk of cheatgrass and juniper spreading across watersheds of the Great Basin. The USDI Bureau of Land Management is using these projections to prioritize watersheds for restoration.

Sage grouse habitat needs

Sage grouse populations and habitat are declining across North America; legal actions seek protection for this species.

▷ Changes in land use and habitat in the Great Basin were assessed for contribution to sage grouse declines in the Great Basin.

▷ Threshold values were identified for sagebrush cover needed by the bird at particular elevations.

▷ U.S. Fish and Wildlife Service is using this information to negotiate with other federal agencies about changes in landscape management to improve conditions for sage grouse and prevent the need for future Endangered Species Act listings.

New models compared historical habitat conditions with current recommendations for sage grouse on the Malheur High Plateau. Findings suggest sage grouse either do not need as much winter habitat as currently recommended or the amount of historical winter habitat has constrained their populations.

Sharing What We've Learned

Station scientists are active in research networks, professional societies, and other forms of collaboration

SCIENCE is meant to be used. Examples below highlight station efforts to share data, conclusions, and tools.

Timely smoke forecasts

The 2011 **Wallow Fire** was Arizona's largest in history, and its effects combined with other fires in the Southwest to produce large regions of unhealthy air.

▷ The National Interagency Fire Coordination Center used station-modeled smoke projections to issue daily smoke forecasts that TV stations relayed to the public.

PNW-FIA database

New database allows users to customize their analyses.

▷ The California Climate Action Registry developed baseline levels of carbon stocks in private forests.

▷ Quick answers were provided for Congressional queries about biomass size distribution and availability of wood supplies from western national forests.

Tracking water contaminants

After severe damage to Japan's Fukushima Daiichi nuclear power plant by the March 2011 earthquake, radioactive contaminants in rivers were tracked by the U.S. Department of Defense.

▷ The tool used to track contaminants, the Incident Command Tool for Protecting Drinking Water (ICWater), was developed by a station scientist and others.

▷ Analyses were shared with emergency managers in Japan to assess public risks of waterborne radioactivity.

Sharing Knowledge and Tools

From research networks and professional societies to local watershed councils—station scientists are active in many different communities. Sharing knowledge and building relationships in these communities helps foster collaboration, knowledge transfer, and education. In 2011,

▷ ~6,920 people participated in symposia, workshops, and webinars sponsored by the station.

▷ ~1,300 people went on field trips led by station researchers.

▷ ~1,770 people participated in conservation education activities sponsored by the station.

◁ Shrub-steppe ecosystems are threatened by invasive species, changing fire regimes, and human development. Photo by Mary Rowland.

Communications—
Print, Web, and Twitter

- 340 total publications. (This includes station series publications, journal articles, books or book chapters, theses and dissertations, and other publications)

- 106,280 hard copies of station publications distributed.

- 43,942 electronic publication downloads from the station's Web site and Treesearch (http://www.treesearch.fs.fed.us).

- 1,906 station publications available online via the station's Web site and Treesearch.

- 9 issues of PNW Science Findings published, about 9,800 copies of each issue distributed.

Web Visitors

- Total number of visits: 75,243 from 155 countries and territories (+ 8.5% from FY2010)

- Total number of unique visitors: 48,851 (+8.7% from fiscal year 2010)

- Total number of page views: 205,698 (about 3 pages viewed per visit)

- Percentage of new visitors: 56.2%

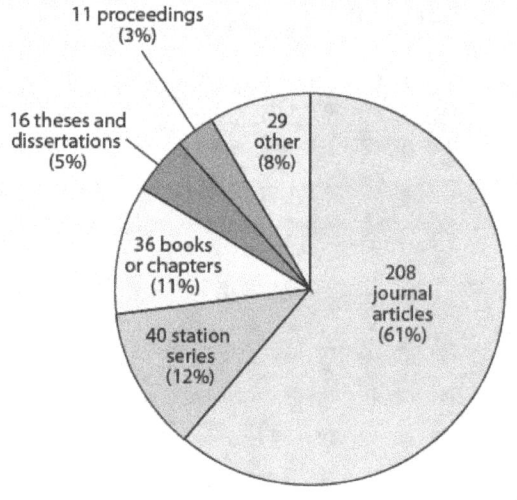

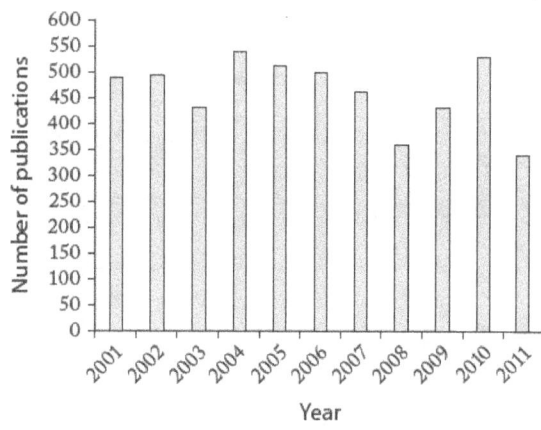

Twitter

The station's Twitter account has 560 followers—up from 250 in 2010. Reporters, natural resource professionals, and nonprofit groups comprise the majority of subscribers, who receive instant electronic alerts (tweets) to station news releases, new publications, and other information.

Our Most Popular Publications

All of the station's publications are available online. Listed below are the 10 publications by station scientists most frequently downloaded from the station's Web site and Forest Service Treesearch site. Some of these publications are decades old but still relevant today.

1. Simulating Fuel Treatment Effects in Dry Forests of the Western United States: Testing the Principles of a Fire-Safe Forest (2011; Canadian Journal of Forest Research)

2. Water, Climate Change, and Forests: Watershed Stewardship for a Changing Climate (2010; PNW-GTR-812)

3. Adaptive Management of Natural Resources: Theory, Concepts, and Management Institutions (2005; PNW-GTR-654)

4. FRAGSTATS: Spatial Pattern Analysis Program for Quantifying Landscape Structure (1995; PNW-GTR-351)

5. A Tale of Two Cedars—International Symposium on Western Redcedar and Yellow-Cedar (2010; PNW-GTR-828)

6. Natural Vegetation of Oregon and Washington (1973; PNW-GTR-008)

7. Nonnative Invasive Plants of Pacific Coast Forests: A Field Guide for Identification (2011; PNW-GTR-817)

8. The Formula Scribner Log Rule (1952; OSN-PNW-078)

9. Advances in Threat Assessment and Their Application to Forest and Rangeland Management (2010; PNW-GTR-802)

10. Ecological Characteristics of Old-Growth Douglas-Fir Forests (1981; PNW-GTR-118)

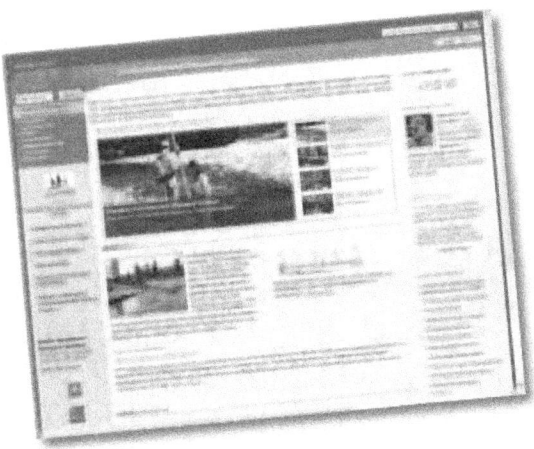

Finances and Workforce

Two sources of funding support the workforce of the Pacific Northwest (PNW) Research Station: federal appropriations, which contribute the greatest percentage of funds, and direct client support, which comes from organizations in need of scientific information.

The numbers below are for the fiscal year **October 1, 2010, to September 30, 2011**

Incoming funding

▷ Base research appropriations: $41.7 million (77%)

▷ Client support: $12.8 million (23%)

▷ Total funding: $54.5 million

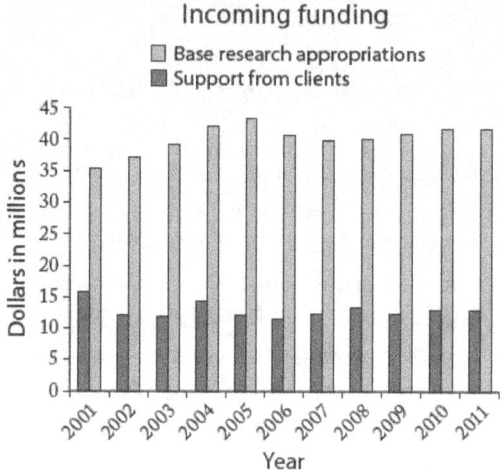

Distribution of funds

▷ Permanent employee cost: $31.1 million (57%)

▷ Support and operations: $13.1 million (24%)

▷ Distributed to cooperators: $10.4 million (19%)

▷ Of $10.4 million to cooperators, 71% went to educational institutions

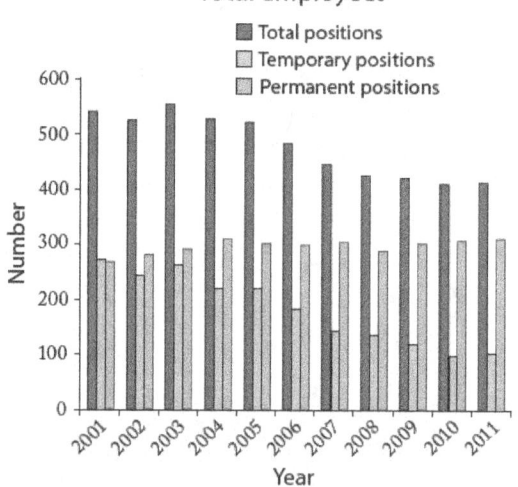

Workforce statistics:

▷ Total station workforce: 413 employees

▷ Permanent workforce: 311 employees

▷ Of the permanent workforce, 85 employees (27%) are scientists

▷ Temporary workforce: 102 employees

Funding Partners for 2011

Cooperators Who Received Funding From the PNW Research Station for Studies

Educational Institutions

Colorado State University
Loyola University
Michigan State University
Oregon State University
Portland State University
Southern Illinois University
Stanford University
State University of New York
University of Alaska (Anchorage)
University of Alaska (Southeast)
University of Hawaii (Hilo)
University of Idaho
University of Minnesota
University of New England
University of Oregon
University of Redlands
University of Washington

Native Tribes

Douglas Indian Association, Juneau, Alaska

Other Federal Agencies

Department of Commerce, National Oceanic and Atmospheric Administration, National Marine Fisheries Service

Department of Commerce, National Oceanic and Atmospheric Administration, National Weather Service, Storm Prediction Center

Department of Defense, Department of the Navy, Systems Management Activity

Department of Defense, U.S. Army Corps of Engineers
Department of the Interior, Bureau of Land Management
Department of the Interior, Geological Survey
Department of the Interior, National Park Service

State Agencies

Arizona Board of Regents
Washington Department of Fish and Wildlife

Municipal and County Agencies

Hillsboro, Oregon, Clean Water Services
Crook County, Oregon

Nongovernmental Organizations

Cascade Land Conservancy
Cascadia Conservation District
Conservation Biology Institute
Earth Systems Institute
Ecotrust
Forest Guild
Hawaii Forest Industry Association
Mount St. Helens Institute
National Council for Air and Stream Improvement, Inc.
Oregon Cultural Heritage Commission
Pacific States Marine Fisheries Commission
Student Conservation Association, Inc.
The Institute for Culture and Ecology
Western Forestry and Conservation Association

Private Industry

Carlson
MacGregor-Bates, Inc.
Seattle Biometrics and Analysis

Clients Who Provided Funding to the PNW Research Station for Studies

Educational Institutions

Oregon State University
University of Alaska (Southeast)
University of California, Berkeley
University of Oregon

Other Federal Agencies

Department of Defense,
U.S. Army Corps of Engineers,
Institute for Water Resources

Department of Defense, U.S. Army,
Joint Base Lewis-McChord

Department of Energy,
Bonneville Power Administration

Department of the Interior,
Bureau of Land Management

Department of the Interior,
Fish and Wildlife Service

Department of the Interior,
Geological Survey

Environmental Protection Agency

National Aeronautics and Space Administration, Goddard Space Flight Center

State Agencies

Oregon Department of Agriculture
Oregon Watershed Enhancement Board

Municipal Agencies

East Bay Regional Park District, California

Nongovernmental Organizations

National Fish and Wildlife Federation
Cascade Land Conservancy
Ecological Research, Inc.
Ecotrust
National Council for Air and Stream Improvement, Inc.
Northwest Power and Conservation Council

Private Industry

Dow Agrosciences

Climate Change

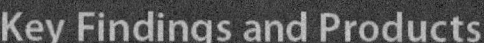

Key Findings and Products

▶ Recent changes in tundra fire regimes, probably in response to climate warming, may cause large amounts of carbon to be released and offset any increases in carbon storage acquired through Arctic greening.

▶ Researchers identify ecosystem processes that can be monitored to track climate-related change in Alaska's forests.

▶ Gene expression atlases for Douglas-fir and two subspecies of big sagebrush have been produced in an effort to identify climate-responsive genes in these species.

▶ New synthesis of physiological and ecological responses of forest trees to climate change is a resource for forest vulnerability and risk assessments.

▶ Maps of predicted vegetation impacts and associated climate change effects on environmental services are available on the Internet.

Arctic fire releases large amounts of stored carbon to the atmosphere

ARCTIC TUNDRA stores large amounts of carbon in cool wet soil that is hundreds to thousands of years old. Fire has been largely absent from this biome for thousands of years, but its frequency and extent are increasing, probably in response to climate warming. The Anaktuvuk River Fire in 2007 burned 645 square miles of Alaska's Arctic slope, making it the largest fire on record for the tundra biome and doubling the cumulative area burned since 1950. The fire released 20 times more carbon to the atmosphere than what is lost annually from undisturbed tundra. This amount is similar in magnitude to the annual net carbon sink for the entire Arctic tundra biome averaged over the last quarter of the 20th century. If fires become a regular disturbance in the Arctic, massive amounts of stored carbon could be released to the atmosphere, leading to further warming of the Earth's climate.

This research is being used to implement measurement techniques that estimate carbon loss in tundra areas. It is also being used by scientists who are initiating studies on the effect of fire disturbance on tree migration into the Arctic.

Contact: Teresa Hollingsworth, thollingsworth@fs.fed.us, Ecological Process and Function Program

Partners: Bonanza Creek Long-Term Ecological Research Program, Marine Biological Laboratory, University of Alaska Fairbanks, University of Florida, USDI Bureau of Land Management Alaska Fire Service

---

Researchers identify options for monitoring climate-related changes in Alaska

AS TEMPERATURES have increased in the boreal forest region of Alaska over the past half century, spruce beetle outbreaks have become larger and more severe, wildfire frequency has increased, permafrost is melting, and boreal tree species in some regions are showing signs of drought stress. Yet impacts on species composition and ecological processes within forests are difficult to monitor.

Use: Federal agencies use assessment to coordinate monitoring.

Researchers from the PNW Research Station and the Department of the Interior examined options for monitoring ecoregional-level change in northern latitudes. Climate-related changes to Alaska's forests that could be monitored include changes in abundance and rarity of vascular plants, wildlife habitat, invasive species, fire risk, fire effects, postfire succession, impacts on forest growth and mortality from insects and diseases, and alterations in carbon pools and fluxes. Although managers of individual parks and refuges often have specific needs that require more targeted

◁ Mount St. Helens, Washington. Photo by Keith Routman.

Olaf Kudgler

As the climate changes, bark beetles and fire pose increasing threats to Alaska's boreal forests.

monitoring, regional level monitoring can help provide context for changes observed within smaller areas.

The researchers published an assessment of the Forest Service's forest inventory program for monitoring climate-related change in Alaska's forests in a 2011 special issue of the journal *Biological Conservation*. This information and an associated 2009 symposium on monitoring in northern latitudes led to the creation of Landscape Conservation Cooperatives, a multiagency effort to coordinate federal monitoring.

Contact: Tara Barrett, tbarrett@fs.fed.us, Threat Characterization and Management Program

Partners: U.S. Geological Survey; USDI Fish and Wildlife Service, National Park Service

Mycorrhizal fungi on roots of tundra shrubs may facilitate postfire establishment of tree seedlings

UNDERSTANDING THE complex mechanisms controlling treeline advance or retreat has important implications for projecting ecosystem responses to direct and indirect effects of global environmental change. A warming climate not only promotes growth of seedlings and mature trees; it also enhances disturbances, such as fire that leads to

further seedling establishment. Critical factors in postfire tree seedling establishment at treeline may be the availability of fungal inoculum for the formation of critical mycorrhizas, which facilitate water and nutrient acquisition.

Preliminary results indicate that most species of tree seedlings can have overlapping fungal taxa with adjacent resprouting shrubs. Also, mature or late-successional fungi may be housed on the roots of tundra shrubs during fire disturbance, which are then available for recruiting seedlings. Synergistic activity between resprouting tundra shrubs and newly established seedlings after fire could either maintain boreal community dynamics at the limit of tree establishment or provide a mechanism for expansion under future scenarios of warming and fire.

Land and fire managers are using these results to help predict future successional trajectories in treeline and tundra ecosystems, and modelers are using these results to more accurately model mechanisms that limit and facilitate tree migration into previously unoccupied areas.

Contact: Teresa Hollingsworth, thollingsworth@fs.fed.us, Ecological Process and Function Program

Partners: Bonanza Creek Long-Term Ecological Research Program, Marine Biological Laboratory, University of Alaska Fairbanks, University of Florida, USDI Bureau of Land Management Alaska Fire Service

Warmer winters likely to expand range of dwarf mistletoe; yellow-cedar continues uphill retreat

CLIMATE IS a key control that regulates where tree species and their pathogens can survive. By analyzing forest inventory data, station scientists found that hemlock dwarf mistletoe, a leading disease agent for western hemlock, is restricted to the warmer southerly and low-elevation forests in Alaska. The absence of dwarf mistletoe in some hemlock forests may be attributed to shorter growing seasons or suggest that snow limits dwarf mistletoe's reproductive dispersal. Both western hemlock and hemlock dwarf mistletoe are projected to benefit from a warmer, less snowy climate. Scientists are projecting the potential distributions of both the tree and disease agent to interpret the health of western hemlock forests during the next century in Alaska.

Western hemlock tree in Alaska killed by a dwarf mistletoe infection.

Continuing research on yellow-cedar populations in southeast Alaska found many dead trees at lower elevations, live trees most common at mid elevation, and that regeneration peaked at higher elevations. These trends are consistent with our understanding that the presence of spring snow is a primary factor in the health and successful regeneration of yellow-cedar. This knowledge is guiding decisions about where to favor this valuable tree through planting and thinning.

Contact: Paul Hennon, phennon@fs.fed.us, Threat Characterization Management Program

Partner: The Nature Conservancy

Changing climates present new threats to the conservation of forest genetic resources

CONSERVING GENETIC resources is important for ensuring sustainability. It allows populations to continue to adapt to new environments and ensures that traits of interest for genetic improvement programs are available. As climates change, populations of native trees may become maladapted and genetic diversity may be lost. Some losses may be minimized by managing stands to be more resistant to threats by using silvicultural treatments such as thinning and prescribed burning. Natural selection and adaptation to changed environments may be promoted in reserves by increasing genetic diversity and promoting gene flow by locating reserves in areas of high environmental heterogeneity, minimizing fragmentation, and using assisted colonization. Collecting seeds, particularly from rare and isolated populations, is another important piece of genetic conservation efforts.

This research highlights the importance of identifying species and populations that are vulnerable to climate change and other threats. It also identifies steps that may help protect and conserve those species and populations. National forests in Oregon and Washington and the Washington Department of Natural Resources have begun working toward these goals by identifying stands for monitoring and seed collection.

Contact: Brad St. Clair, bstclair@fs.fed.us, Land and Watershed Management Program

Partner: Oregon State University

Geneticists make progress identifying genes responsible for climate tolerance in Douglas-fir and big sagebrush

MANY FOREST and range plants are finely attuned to their local climate, making it necessary to match seed sources with planting locations. From ecological and economic perspectives, the adaptability of the plants is critical. Forest Service and university geneticists are working to identify genes that enable certain trees and plants to tolerate and adapt to climatic extremes. This knowledge will enable nursery managers to deliver locally adapted, genetically appropriate materials for restoration even as the climate changes.

Gene expression atlases have been developed for two subspecies of big sagebrush, which together include 21,000 genes. Similar efforts in Douglas-fir have identified over 38,000. These atlases are being used in conjunction with common garden studies to identify the relevance of differential gene expression and genetic polymorphism in climatic adaptation. Candidate adaptive genes will be targeted for

detailed study so that the genes responsible for climate tolerance and adaptability can be identified and managed in future forests.

Contact: Rich Cronn, rcronn@fs.fed.us, Land and Watershed Management Program

Partners: Brigham Young University, Oregon State University, Utah State University, USDA Forest Service Rocky Mountain Research Station

---

Understanding physical processes of tree development offers clues to tree response to warmer climate

A TREE undergoes many physical changes during its life. Leaf physiology, wood structure, mechanical properties, reproductive ability, and interactions with herbivores and pathogens are just some of the features that change as a seedling grows to maturity. Many of these changes are presumed to allow trees to acclimate to the environment and endure for millennia. Understanding these processes may be key to anticipating their response to warmer climates.

A new book, *Size- and Age-Related Changes in Tree Structure and Function*, highlights some implications of these size- and age-related changes for commercial forestry plantations with shortened rotational ages. It also discusses how current and future forests will likely respond to climate and other environmental changes.

Contact: Rick Meinzer, frneinzer@fs.fed.us, Ecological Process and Function Program

Partners: Oregon State University, University of California Berkeley

For more information: Meinzer, F.C.; Lachen-bruch, B.; Dawson, T.E., eds. 2011. Size- and age-related changes in tree structure and function. Tree Physiology 4, Springer Science and Business Media. http://www.springer.com/life+sciences/forestry/book/978-94-007-1241-6.

Richard Cronn

Douglas-fir needles are flash-frozen in liquid nitrogen to preserve the status of gene expression at that instant. Back in the lab, researchers will look for adaptive genes that may help the species adapt to climate change.

Scientists synthesize knowledge of tree responses to climate change

SEVERAL DECADES of research exist on the potential responses of trees and forests to climate-related stresses. Station scientists and colleagues at Oregon State University synthesized more than 400 research articles addressing physiological and ecological responses of trees and forests to variations in climate and associated stresses and disturbance agents. Although based on an international body of research, the synthesis highlights potential climate changes and responses from species and ecosystems in the Pacific Northwest. It is organized around key themes: elevated levels of atmospheric carbon dioxide, temperature, precipitation, fire, pests, and their interactions, and discusses vulnerabilities and risks from a forestry management perspective. The authors identify options for silvicultural and genetic approaches to managing for forest adaptation.

The synthesis is a resource when conducting forest vulnerability and risk assessments and planning adaptation strategies. Researchers and modelers may also find it useful when developing and testing hypotheses or models of forest development and production under various future climatic conditions.

Contact: Paul D. Anderson, pdanderson@fs.fed.us, Land and Watershed Management Program

Partners: Oregon Department of Forestry; Oregon Forest Resources Institute; Oregon State University; Taskforce on Adapting Forests to Climate Change; USDA Forest Service Pacific Northwest Region; USDI Bureau of Land Management, National Park Service; Washington Department of Natural Resources

For more information: Chmuraa, D.J.; Anderson, P.D.; Howe, G.T. [et al.]. 2011. Forest responses to climate change in the northwestern United States: ecophysiological foundations for adaptive management. Forest Ecology and Management. 261: 1121–1142.

Connie Harrington

Different populations of Douglas-fir burst bud at different times. The seedling in the foreground has not burst bud while the one from a different population behind it has begun to grow.

Spring budburst model projects timing of budburst under different winter conditions

MANY PLANT species and different populations within species have evolved so that their spring budburst coincides with environmental conditions conducive to growth. Plants sense cold and warm temperatures during winter so that they can tell when winter has passed and it is safe to burst bud. New growth that emerges too early in the spring, for example, could be killed by a later cold snap. Climate change has the potential to alter the signals that plants use, thereby changing the timing of budburst. Models are needed to predict the timing of budburst under different types of winter

conditions. Because different populations have evolved to survive in different winter environments, the models need to be sensitive to how each population determines when it is safe to burst bud. Station scientists developed a model to predict the timing of budburst for populations of Douglas-fir, the major tree species in northwest forests.

The budburst model has been published so that it can be used by other scientists and land managers. It can be used to help assess climate impacts on scales ranging from individual trees to the entire range of coast Douglas-fir.

Contact: Peter Gould, pgould@fs.fed.us, Land and Watershed Management Program

Partners: Oregon State University, USDI Bureau of Land Management, Washington Department of Natural Resources

Maps summarizing projected change in global and North America vegetation available online

UNTIL NOW, the sheer volume of information generated by the MC1 dynamic global vegetation model simulations has created a bottleneck when it comes to analysis, limiting its utility to managers, regulators, and policymakers. The MC1 model is routinely used in North America to predict vegetation impacts associated with climate-change projections to the year 2100, as well as associated changes to ecosystem services such as water availability and carbon sequestration. When using 5- by 5-mile grid cells, roughly 350,000 cells cover North America, and MC1 outputs for each cell include over 50 measures for each of three climate realizations (from multiple general-circulation models) and three carbon-emission scenarios, and data are output monthly for a 200-year simulation. The MC1 user community spans a large number of international, federal, state, local, and nongovernmental organizations.

Now, the most commonly requested summary map products from the global and North American MC1 simulations are available to this community for viewing and download from the DataBasin Web site at http://databasin.org/.

Contact: Keith Reynolds, kreynolds@fs.fed.us, Ecological Process and Function Program

Partners: Conservation Biology Institute, Environmental Systems Research Institute, Oregon State University

---

New NetMap module facilitates climate change planning at the watershed level

THE EFFECTS of climate change differ depending on local conditions such as topography and aspect, making it difficult for natural resource managers and decisionmakers to plan ahead. To remove some of the guesswork, Forest Service scientists and collaborators developed NetMap, a tool to help users determine where a suite of ecological processes that influence aquatic ecosystems are likely to occur in a particular landscape. Now, researchers have added a feature to NetMap so users can further scale likely climate-change impacts to specific watersheds in national forests of the Pacific Northwest. Changes in the pattern and amount of streamflow, water temperatures, and wildfire frequency and magnitude are the main impacts considered. Results from this analysis can be exported to Google Earth to better show where changes are most likely to occur.

Use: Five national forests use new projections to plan for climate change.

NetMap and the associated downscaled projections were shared with five national forests in the Pacific Northwest in 2011. National forest personnel are using the projections to help develop management strategies and programs to respond to climate change and to develop

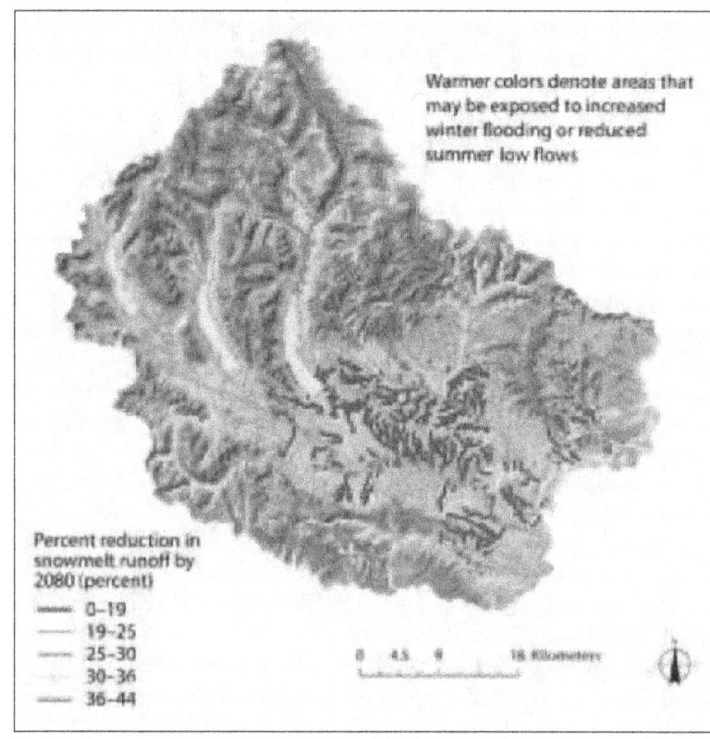

Warmer colors denote areas that may be exposed to increased winter flooding or reduced summer low flows

Percent reduction in snowmelt runoff by 2080 (percent)

- 0–19
- 19–25
- 25–30
- 30–36
- 36–44

0   4.5   9   18 Kilometers

Global climate models indicate that areas of highest elevation are predicted to have the greatest reduction in snowmelt runoff by 2080 in the upper Yakima basin, Washington. In NetMap, downscaled predictions from global climate models are routed downstream, creating a fish-eye view of potential climate impacts that include increased winter flooding or reduced summer low flows.

Field crew inventory a study plot on the Wenatchee National Forest.

more strategic monitoring plans. All national forests in the Pacific Northwest will have NetMap and the climate change module by September 2012. The Bureau of Land Management has contracted the PNW Research Station to make NetMap available for selected districts in Oregon, as has the Tongass National Forest in Alaska.

Contact: Gordon Reeves, greeves@fs.fed.us, Land and Watershed Management Program

Partners: Earth Systems Institute, University of Washington

How to get it: http://netmaptools.org/

Science-management partnership facilitates management adapted to climate change

AS PART OF an agency-wide effort, station scientists have been collaborating with national forest managers and other agencies to ensure that climate change will be addressed effectively on federal land. Through a science-management partnership, they have developed scientific principles, processes, and tools for communicating about climate science, conducting assessments of the vulnerability of natural resources to climate change, and developing adaptation strategies and tactics that ensure sustainability of resources in a warmer climate.

In the Pacific Northwest, scientists and land managers have developed (1) a vulnerability assessment and climate change adaptation strategy for Olympic National Forest and Olympic National Park, (2) a national adaptation guidebook for national forests, and (3) the North Cascadia Adaptation Partnership (http://northcascadia.org), which is implementing education, vulnerability assessment, and adaptation planning across two national forests and two national parks in Washington state.

This effort is helping national forests follow the U.S. Forest Service Climate Change Roadmap and addresses specific elements in the Climate Change Scorecard, which is used by national forests to track progress on the integration of climate change into their operations.

Contact: David L. Peterson, peterson@fs.fed.us, Threat Characterization and Management Program

Partners: University of Washington Climate Impacts Group, USDI National Park Service

For more information: Peterson, D.L.; Millar, C.I.; Joyce, L.A. [et al.]. 2011. Responding to climate change in national forests: a guidebook for developing adaptation options. Gen. Tech. Rep. PNW-GTR-855. Portland, OR: U.S. Department of Agriculture, Forest Service, Pacific Northwest Research Station. 109 p.

Community Sustainability

Key Findings and Products

▷ Forest Service projects funded by the American Recovery and Reinvestment Act produced short- and long-term jobs and other social, economic, and health benefits in economically distressed rural communities while helping the agency meet its forest management goals.

▷ Comprehensive report on wood-to-energy projects guides USDA initiative to build a forest restoration economy.

▷ Airborne LIDAR sampling provides a tool for efficiently estimating forest bioenergy supply near communities in interior Alaska.

▷ Partnerships expand agency capacity and build community ties.

▷ Recreation activities in national forests burn billions of calories each year, helping combat obesity.

 **Tools**

Tribal Climate Change Project Profiles

Description:
With their close cultural and economic relationship to the land, American Indian and Alaska Native tribes face disproportionate risks associated with climate change. Station scientists have developed information tools to help build awareness of the unique problems faced by tribal stakeholders in addressing natural resource issues, as well as their innovative approaches to adaptation. These profiles summarize climate change mitigation and adaptation projects implemented around the United States to share success stories and provide examples for others to learn from. In addition, profiles include information on available resources, key contacts, and government programs that can provide services or grants.

Use:
The Lummi Nation and Swinomish, Coquille, and Nez Perce Tribes have all participated in the process, using the method to initiate adaptation planning and projects that anticipate further climate change. The collaborative model is being replicated in Forest Service research stations across the agency as part of an all-station tribal climate change initiative.

How to get it:
http://tribalclimate.uoregon.edu/tribal-profiles/

Contact:
Ellen Donoghue, edonoghue@fs.fed.us,
Goods, Services, and Values Program

Web Site: Green Cities—Good Health

Description:
This Web site concisely summarizes the benefits of urban trees and green spaces, based on more than 1,700 scientific articles. Key findings are presented for multiple audiences, such as resource managers in local government, conservation groups, and nongovernmental organizations. The research evidence about the benefits of the human experience of nature in cities indicates proximity to nature can lead to stress reduction, healing, better learning and work productivity, and improved social dynamics in communities. All of these findings have broad implications, from human capital enhancement, to community cohesion, to economic costs and benefits.

Use:
This project provides a suite of evidence-based products that explain the diverse benefits associated with having well-managed nature in cities and towns.

How to get it:
http://www.greenhealth.washington.edu/

Contact:
Dale Blahna, dblahna@fs.fed.us,
Goods, Services, and Values Program

◁ Loading kiln-dried lumber at dry kiln and restacker facility in Tamarack, Idaho, a project funded by the American Recovery and Reinvestment Act. Photo by Jessi Kershner.

Investment in rural communities created social and economic benefits

THE AMERICAN Recovery and Reinvestment Act (ARRA) was signed in 2009 as part of a nationwide stimulus to create jobs for Americans in economically distressed locations across the country. The Forest Service received $1.15 billion in ARRA stimulus money for recovery projects intended to increase economic opportunities in local communities, while addressing the agency's mission of sustaining the health of public forests and grasslands. Did these investments make a difference in rural areas?

A station scientist led an evaluation of the social and economic impacts of ARRA-funded projects in eight economically distressed rural areas across the United States. Her team found that Forest Service investments in these projects helped meet the goals of the Recovery Act and demonstrated that Forest Service investments in rural communities can have far-reaching social and economic benefits for local residents, as well as positive outcomes for the agency.

An American Recovery and Reinvestment Act project on the Rogue River-Siskiyou National Forest enabled some contractors to stay in business through the recession.

Some of these outcomes included short and long-term job creation, revitalizing existing economic sectors, stimulating new economic capacity, and accomplishing restoration work of a type and at a scale that would not have happened otherwise.

Contact: Susan Charnley, scharnley@fs.fed.us, Goods, Services, and Values Program

Partners: Auburn University; Fort Lewis College; Southern Oregon University; University of Oregon; USDA Forest Service Northern Research Station, Southern Research Station

Citation: Charnley, S.; Jakes, P.; Schelhas, J., tech. coords. 2011. Socioeconomic assessment of Forest Service American Recovery and Reinvestment Act projects: eight case studies. Gen. Tech. Rep. PNW-GTR-831. Portland, OR: U.S. Department of Agriculture, Forest Service, Pacific Northwest Research Station. 168 p. http://www.treesearch.fs.fed.us/pubs/37857

Lessons learned from past wood-to-energy project may help current effort

AS OIL PRICES climb, rural communities struggle, and forests accumulate fuel, the pressure to address these challenges becomes more insistent. An interagency wood-to-energy program could provide a solution that would benefit the American people in several ways, including reducing or completely offsetting costs of forest restoration and fire-risk-reduction activities; reducing the use of fossil fuels for production of electricity, thermal energy, and liquid fuels; and helping to stabilize the economies of rural communities. Recognizing this, Department of Agriculture Secretary Thomas Vilsack stated a goal of advancing forest restoration efforts through woody biomass utilization.

A station scientist was asked to contribute to this effort by developing a comprehensive report on lessons learned from previous wood-to-energy projects. The report yielded recommendations that will help the Department of Agriculture form new partnerships and maximize opportunities to pursue development of wood to energy.

Contact: Jamie Barbour, jbarbour01@fs.fed.us, Focused Science Delivery Program

Station scientists are contributing to various efforts examining the feasibility of wood-to-energy projects. Above, a truck unloads woody biomass that will be used to produce electricity at the Blue Lake power plant in California.

LIDAR used to estimate biomass supply near interior Alaska communities

REMOTE RURAL communities in interior Alaska generally rely on fossil fuel to meet their power and heating needs. Diesel prices increased 83 percent from 2000 to 2005, however, and utility costs can amount to more than a third of a household's income. Wood-based energy may be a viable alternative, but estimates of available forest biomass are needed before comprehensive plans for bioenergy production can be developed. Interior Alaska has relatively few roads, making it difficult to measure biomass availability over a large area using conventional ground-based sampling methods. Therefore, researchers tested the precision of data collected by aircraft equipped with LIDAR (airborne laser scanners) and used it in conjunction with data from sparse field plots.

The LIDAR sampling approach estimated total biomass with an 8 percent level of precision, indicating that the 200,000-hectare study in the upper Tanana valley contained 8.1 million (± 0.7 million) metric tons of biomass. They found that precision increased when plot locations were more accurately located, when larger plots were measured, and when additional smaller trees in the ground plots were measured.

This study indicates that airborne LIDAR sampling can be useful in planning bioenergy development in interior Alaska. In regions with very limited road access, an approach to field plot selection within accessible areas can be used to ensure that representative plots are measured to develop robust LIDAR biomass estimates.

Contact: Hans Andersen, handersen@fs.fed.us, Resource Monitoring and Assessment Program

Partner: Oregon State University

Partnerships expand agency capacity and build community ties

THE FOREST SERVICE has responded to declining budgets and diverse public demands by increasing its reliance on collaboration with partners. A station scientist developed a conceptual framework of recreation partnerships to help identify some of the implications of these interactions for accomplishing agency goals. The scientist found that partnership durability can be enhanced through strong personal connections, clear communication, and transparent expectations and roles. In some cases, strong relationships that balance partner priorities and agency goals can yield greater outcomes, provide access to new partnership networks, and supply additional resources. However, the assumption that partnerships provide free services that can simply replace agency functions with minimal investment can be problematic. Partnerships actually require considerable effort and investment in fostering relations and ensuring followthrough.

Contact: Lee Cerveny, lcerveny@fs.fed.us, Goods, Services, and Values Program

Partner: Southern Illinois University, Carbondale

Houses with street trees are less prone to crime

A STUDY IN Portland, Oregon, found that houses fronted with more street trees experience lower crime rates, as do houses with large yard trees. These results hold for total-crime rates as well as specific property crimes such as vandalism and burglary. Trees may reduce crime by signaling that a neighborhood is well cared for. These findings are consistent with the "broken window" hypothesis, which maintains that signs of neighborhood neglect, such as graffiti or untended yards, send a signal to potential criminals that the area is run down and that residents may not take steps to protect it. However, yards that contain many small trees had higher crime rates. Small trees and shrubs can obstruct views, making it easier for criminals to hide. Other view-obstructing features, such as fences, were also associated with higher crime rates. This finding underlines the tradeoff homeowners must make between security and privacy.

The City of Portland's Crime Prevention Program is incorporating these findings in its

Use: Portland's Crime Prevention Program uses finding to educate homeowners.

Megan McGuire

Volunteers build a trail on the Sandy River Delta, Oregon.

education and outreach work with local service providers, public safety activists, neighborhood associations, and other community members. This study received considerable media coverage. The Associated Press picked it up, leading to over 300 stories in newspapers and magazines and on television and radio. Outlets include the *Washington Post, USA Today,* Associated Press, UPI, *Daily Mail* (England), NPR, CBS, NBC, FOX, ESPN, *Discovery News, Science Daily,* and *Landscape Architecture Magazine.*

Contact: Geoffrey Donovan, gdonovan@fs.fed.us, Goods, Services, and Values Program

Partner: USDA Forest Service Southern Research Station

Urban trees linked to better birth outcomes

A RECENT STUDY by the PNW Research Station explored the link between tree cover and human birth outcomes in Portland, Oregon. Scientists compared tree cover around the homes of nearly

Use:
Alliance for Community Trees in Maryland includes findings in education campaign.

6,000 women who delivered babies in Portland in 2006 and 2007. They found that women in homes with more canopy cover within 50 meters were less likely to have an under-weight baby. Proximity to private open space also reduced this risk.

To rule out other possible effects, scientists controlled for over 100 variables including the mother's age, ethnic background, household income, and education level. Previous research has shown that exposure to nature can reduce stress levels, which suggests that trees may improve birth outcomes by reducing maternal stress.

As the first study to demonstrate the link between the natural environment and reproductive health, this information supports urban planning and policymaking by providing specific examples of the positive impact trees have on community well-being. Findings are directly relevant to the Mult-nomah County Health Department's mission to enhance the health of the people in the community.

The Alliance for Community Trees in Maryland is using the study in its education and outreach campaign. These findings were reported widely

Researchers found a relationship between large urban trees, lower crime rates, and higher birth weights.

in the media, including several newspapers in the Pacific Northwest, radio interviews, and online sources.

Contact: Geoffrey Donovan, gdonovan@fs.fed.us, Goods, Services, and Values Program

Partners: Drexel University, Multnomah County Health Department, National Institute of Standards and Technology

Annual recreation on national forests burns 289 billion calories

DESPITE THE known benefits of exercise, two-thirds of Americans do not get enough. Children average 30 hours a week in front of television or computer screens, and one in five are obese. But humans still have a psychological affinity for nature, and physical activity—especially outdoors—can contribute greatly to a healthy lifestyle. Scientists evaluated the public health benefits provided by national forests by estimating the calorie expenditure of visitors recreating on national forest lands. They found that national forests receive over 170 million recreation visits per year, featuring a range of physical activities including hiking, camping, skiing, wildlife viewing,

Keith Routman

Hikers stay in shape on the Mount Hood National Forest.

Forests near Sitka, Alaska, sequester more CO$_2$ than city produces

SITKA, ALASKA, has substantial hydroelectric resources, limited driving distances, and a relatively mild maritime climate, all suggesting strong opportunities for the city to lessen its carbon footprint. Station scientists evaluated human-caused carbon dioxide (CO$_2$) emissions from Sitka, Alaska, and compared results with the estimated carbon sequestration potential of forest ecosystems on Baranof Island in southeast Alaska. They found that forest carbon sequestration was conservatively estimated to be about twice that of human-caused emissions from Sitka. Several factors could reduce Sitka's carbon footprint even further, including a proposed expansion of the Blue Lake hydroelectric facility near Sitka, increased use of wood energy for residential heating, use of electric vehicles, and adoption of energy conservation practices throughout the community.

Contact: David Nicholls, dlnicholls@fs.fed.us, Goods, Services, and Values Program

and fishing. These and other activities burned more than 289 billion calories, of which nearly 264 billion were expended by adults and about 26 billion were expended by youth. Expressed in terms of food, those calories equal enough french fries placed end-to-end to reach the moon and back, twice.

The annual energy expenditures from national forest recreation are equivalent to the exercise necessary for 6.8 million adults and 317,000 youths to meet the Centers for Disease Control and Prevention guidelines regarding daily aerobic physical activity for a year. The President's Taskforce on Childhood Obesity report called for continued investments in a wide range of outdoor recreation venues, such as national parks, forests, refuges, and other public lands as one approach to lessening childhood obesity. As a result, public health officials, policymakers, and recreation planners all need information on how outdoor recreation on public lands influence opportunities for physical activity.

Contact: Jeff Kline, jkline@fs.fed.us, Goods, Services, and Values Program

Partner: Oregon State University

David Nicholls

Forests near Sitka, Alaska, sequester more carbon dioxide than the city produces, and opportunities exist for the city to further reduce its carbon emissions.

Evaluation of NEPA processes finds that team harmony and empowered leaders lead to success

THE FOREST SERVICE has struggled to understand why its planning procedures associated with the National Environmental Policy Act (NEPA) are sometimes inefficient,

Use: *Forest Service develops new NEPA training based on findings.*

perform poorly in the eyes of the public, and fail to deliver outputs that advance agency mission. Looking for solutions, researchers examined a representative sample of NEPA processes conducted by the agency between 2007 and 2009. They examined interdisciplinary team leaders' perceptions of the following outcomes: achievement of agency goals and NEPA mandates, process efficiency, public relations, and team outcomes. The most consistent predictors of positive outcomes in meeting NEPA requirements were team harmony and a team leader who felt empowered. The results suggest the importance of genuine concern and respect for participating members of the public, as well as effective interagency coordination.

Forest Service leadership and others who regularly work with NEPA planning are using this information to develop new training sessions for managing interdisciplinary teams.

Contact: David Seesholtz, dseesholtz@fs.fed.us, Focused Science Delivery Program

Partner: Virginia Tech

Tom Iracis

Team harmony and an empowered leader were the most consistent predictors of positive outcomes in meeting NEPA requirements.

NEPA processes influenced by external social pressures

THE NATIONAL Environmental Policy Act (NEPA) requires an environmental assessment (EA) or a more involved environmental impact statement (EIS) to be completed before federal action can occur, if there is potential for the activity to negatively affect the environment

Researchers found that the reasons for preparing an EIS were in many cases not clearly related to the environmental focus of NEPA and its regulations. The NEPA for the 21st Century Initiative found that practitioners followed several themes for preferring an EIS over an EA that went beyond the considerations outlined in official regulations. These themes included threat of litigation and ability to withstand legal challenges, level of public controversy, and the ability to incur a significant impact.

The possibility that a NEPA practitioner may consider these factors is being built into a risk-management framework under development. This framework will help practitioners determine an appropriate course of action for accomplishing their NEPA responsibilities.

Contact: David Seesholtz, dseesholtz@fs.fed.us, Focused Science Delivery Program

Partners: State University of New York, Virginia Tech

Fire and Smoke

Key Findings and Products

▶ A new book, *The Landscape Ecology of Fire*, analyzes wildfire in western North America at the spatial scales most relevant for management, with an emphasis on how fire regimes may evolve in an era of rapid global change.

▶ Intensive thinning treatments are needed to reduce crown fire hazard in dry forests of the western United States.

▶ The MC1 Fire Forecasting System provides the basis for experimental forecasts of annual firefighting expenditures and optimal timing for prescribed fire.

Tools

Fuel Characteristic Classification System (FCCS) v. 2.2

Description:

The Fuel Characteristic Classification System (FCCS) was designed to build and catalog fuelbeds by using inventoried fuel data, photo series, or literature. Fuelbeds span the canopy to the ground and have been mapped for the continental United States. The system predicts surface fire behavior including reaction intensity, flame length, and rate of spread; and surface fire behavior, crown fire, and available fuel potential using a 9-point index. Version 2.2 was released in 2011 with refined fire behavior equations, a total carbon calculator, and options for both metric and English units. Station scientists are working with the University of Aveiro, Portugal, and the University of Alcala, Spain, to build FCCS fuelbeds representing Portugal and the world.

Use:

The FCCS is used to build and characterize fuels for specified areas at any scale of interest. FCCS fuelbeds have been created for the Okanogan-Wenatchee National Forest, central Oregon, the Lake Tahoe Basin, and the U.S. Department of Energy's Savannah River Site. The associated fire behavior predictions and total carbon represented by the fuelbeds for these areas also have been mapped. This information is being used for fire hazard planning and evaluating fuels treatment effectiveness.

How to get it:
http://www.fs.fed.us/pnw/fera/fccs/

Contact:
Roger Ottmar, rottmar@fs.fed.us, Threat Characterization and Management Program

◁ June 2011 Wallow Fire, Apache-Sitgreaves National Forest, Arizona. Photo by Jayson Coil.

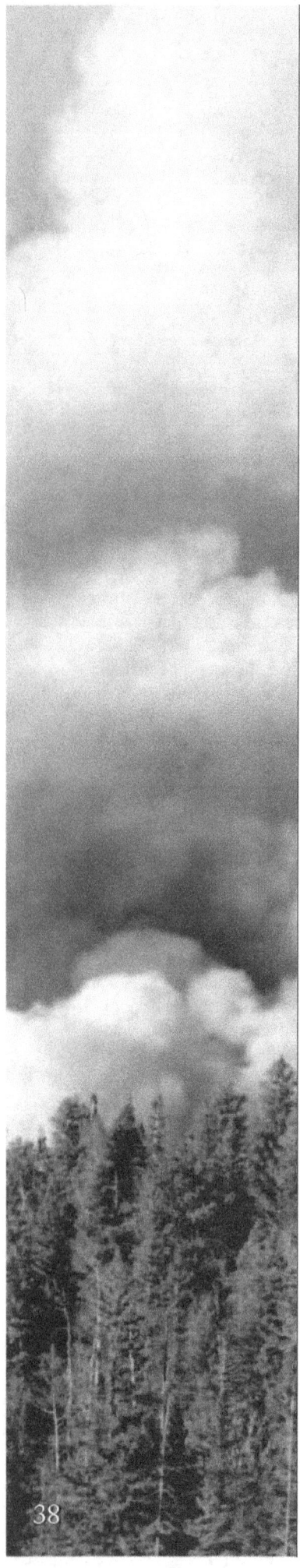

Tools

Fuel Characteristics Classification System/ Forest Vegetation Simulator Postprocessor

Description:

The Forest Vegetation Simulator (FVS) is used to predict forest stand dynamics. It is used extensively throughout the United States. The Fire and Fuels Extension to FVS, when combined with the Fuel Characteristic Classification System (FCCS), has the potential to model fire effects and succession more realistically and with higher resolution. Postprocessors are stand-alone applications that extend the capabilities of a model. This new postprocessor will integrate the effects of silvicultural and surface fuel treatments, using realistic fuels and making the fuels component more visible, user friendly, and flexible within the modeling system.

Use:

The FVS is the standard model used by various government agencies including the USDA Forest Service, USDI Bureau of Land Management, and USDI Bureau of Indian Affairs. The new interface provided by this postprocessor will allow managers to more accurately determine the outcomes of fuel treatments, especially with respect to duration of treatment effectiveness.

How to get it:

Tool will be distributed with the FVS program, or download from http://www.fs.fed.us/fmsc/fvs/software/postprocessors.php

Contact:

Morris C. Johnson, mcjohnson@fs.fed.us, Threat Characterization and Management Program

---

Modeling the Effect of Fire on Aquatic Systems

Description:

These models predict the potential of fire to alter critical in-stream salmon habitat by modeling a fire's potential to facilitate delivery of sediment and large wood to stream channels. The models are also used to consider road impacts following fires.

The analysis tools incorporate the physical attributes of hillslopes and of stream channels with models of fire behavior and fire intensity across the landscape. These tools are designed to be used with output from FlamMap—a fire behavior mapping and analysis program. The models are available in the ArcGIS version of NetMap and some portion of them will become available in a Web browser in 2012.

Use:

These tools are intended for land and natural resource management.

How to get it:

http://www.netmaptools.org/

Contact:

Rebecca Flitcroft, rflitcroft@fs.fed.us, Land and Watershed Management Program

Partner:

Earth Systems Institute

◁ June 2011 Wallow Fire, Apache-Sitgreaves National Forest, Arizona. Photo by Jayson Coil.

New book analyzes landscape fire regimes across western North America

UNDERSTANDING wildfire dynamics across a broad range of spatial scales is critical in an era of rapid climate change. Ecological fire science is most complex at intermediate scales (e.g., watersheds or national forest districts). The recently published book *The Landscape Ecology of Fire* presents new work on the theoretical context of landscape fire, including cross-scale analyses; fire climatology specifically applied to landscapes; effects of fire on biogeochemistry, wildlife populations, and other ecosystem elements; and management and the human dimension of landscape fire in a warming climate. For example, cross-scale analysis of fire regimes from watersheds to ecoregions suggests that shifting controls on fire occurrence and spread (climate, topography, fuels) can be quantified and projected into new climate regimes. On the human side, regional-scale adaptation strategies are presented along with a West-wide analysis of the effects of population growth on wilderness fire management.

The book is written for university students, agency scientists, and land managers with jurisdictions from local watersheds to broad ecoregions (e.g., Forest Service regions). Two new lines of research stem from this book: the ecohydrology of fire and landscape fire theory.

Contact: Don McKenzie, donaldmckenzie@fs.fed.us, Threat Characterization and Management Program

Partners: University of Arizona, University of Washington, USDA Forest Service Rocky Mountain Research Station

For more information: McKenzie, D.; Miller, C.; Falk, D.A., eds. 2011. The landscape ecology of fire. Ecological Studies. V. 213. New York: Springer Science. 312 p.

Simulating fuel treatments on 40,000 stands yields quantitative guidelines for resource managers

DRY FOREST ecosystems prevalent in western North America historically exhibited high-frequency and low- to moderate-severity fire regimes. Several decades of fire exclusion have made these forests more susceptible to active crown fire and higher burn severity. Fuel treatments are

A 2011 study provided quantitative guidelines for thinning and fuel treatments in the western United States.

often implemented to reduce fire hazard caused by increased stem densities in low- to moderate-severity fire regimes. With millions of hectares of dry forests in the western United States requiring fuel treatment, forest and fire managers need information to support science-based decisionmaking for fuel management.

In the largest study ever evaluating the effectiveness of fuel treatments, researchers used simulation results from over 40,000 stands to infer that thinning to 50 to 100 trees per acre followed by prescribed burning to remove slash was the most effective treatment combination to reduce crown fire hazard in dry forest types throughout the western United States. These quantitative guidelines for thinning and fuel treatment provide resource managers and fire managers with the scientific basis for reducing stand densities and surface fuels.

This study received significant media coverage; it was featured in Greenwire, Land Letter, National Public Radio, and the *Arizona Daily Sun*, among others.

Contact: Morris C. Johnson, mcjohnson@fs.fed.us, Threat Characterization and Management Program
Partner: University of Washington

Fire forecasting system provides basis for expenditure forecast and timing of prescribed fire

STATION SCIENTISTS produce continuously updated 7-month forecasts of fire potential and drought for the conterminous United States for use in fire management planning. As of 2010, these high-resolution forecast models are routinely run at the Arctic Region Supercomputer Center in partnership with the University of Alaska. Along with summary maps of predicted drought and fire potential, the MC1 Fire Forecasting System now also predicts area burned, the moisture content of several live and dead fuel classes, and measures of potential fire behavior including rate of spread, fireline intensity, and the energy release component. These detailed data are being provided as input to two new experimental forecasting systems under development by researchers at the Rocky Mountain Research Station and Western Regional Climate Center (WRCC).

The Rocky Mountain Research Station is using MC1 burn forecasts to predict annual firefighting expenditures with results that are significantly better than the professional judgments currently made at the National Interagency Fire Center. The WRCC is using MC1 forecasts of fuel moisture and fire behavior to predict optimal timing for prescribed fire and posting them monthly to a WRCC-sponsored Web site.

Contact: Jim Lenihan, jlenihan@fs.fed.us, and Ray Drapek, rdrapek@fs.fed.us, Ecological Process and Function Program

Partners: Desert Research Institute, Oregon State University, National Interagency Fire Center, University of Alaska, USDA Forest Service Rocky Mountain Research Station, Western Regional Climate Center

◁ June 2011 Wallow Fire, Apache-Sitgreaves National Forest, Arizona. Photo by Jayson Coil.

Jayson Coil

June 2011 Wallow Fire, Apache-Sitgreaves National Forest, Arizona.

Station expertise helped predict smoke from Southwest fires

THIS YEAR, numerous large wildfires burned across the southwestern United States. Fueled by historically low fuel moistures, these fires exhibited explosive growth and grew to unprecedented size—the Wallow Fire is the largest in contemporary Arizona history. The smoke from these fires created a significant public health challenge, blanketing large swaths of Arizona and New Mexico with unhealthy air quality conditions.

Use: National Interagency Fire Coordination Center uses expertise to issue daily smoke forecasts.

Federal, state, tribal, and local government agencies pooled resources to create a coordinated smoke and health effects outlook that was disseminated to the public. Expertise from the PNW Research Station was requested and was a key component of this effort. Station scientists provided a core set of customized advanced smoke modeling results and expert analyses to the group on a daily basis. Their efforts were instrumental in determining the daily smoke outlook.

These reports were linked to the Web site that lists information about all active fires in the Nation (Inciweb) and accessed thousands of times by involved agencies and the public. The reports were redistributed by up to 20 agencies that coordinated their message through daily consultations. The smoke outlooks were also picked up by television stations around the region and were used by the public for such things as rescheduling sporting events to avoid times of peak smoke.

Contact: Sim Larkin, larkin@fs.fed.us, Threat Characterization and Management Program

Partners: Desert Research Institute; Lawrence Livermore National Laboratory's National Atmospheric Release Advisory Center; Mazama Science; National Weather Service; Sonoma Technology, Inc.; USDA Forest Service Southwestern Region Fire and Aviation Management, Wildland Fire Research Development and Application

Analysis of atmospheric thermal troughs suggests why they cause more active fire behavior

THERMAL TROUGHS are atmospheric structures found along the west coast of the United States, characterized by high surface temperatures and low pressure. They typically form along the coast or in Oregon's Willamette Valley and eventually move eastward across the Cascade Range. They are associated with active, highly variable fire behavior at all times, but most notably as they cross the ridge of the Cascades. Analysis of historical thermal troughs using atmospheric models revealed characteristic wind patterns aloft, patterns that are not detectable on the ground but capable of intensifying winds and fire behavior. Continuing, more detailed analysis of a small set of thermal trough events and the associated fire behavior is clarifying finer scale structure and the forces causing the wind patterns.

A prototype Web page has been created and shared with the Northwest fire weather community for their use and evaluation. The numerical prediction maps and atmospheric cross-sections displayed were chosen based on ongoing discussions with the National Weather Service and the Northwest Interagency Coordination Center.

Contact: Brian Potter, bpotter@fs.fed.us, Threat Characterization and Management Program

Partners: National Weather Service, Northwest Interagency Coordination Center, University of Washington, USDA Forest Service Washington office

For more information: http://www.atmos.washington.edu/mm5rt/firewatch.html

Summer prescribed burns can reduce acorn production by Oregon white oak

THE OREGON white oak is a sun-loving tree. Without fire, conifers increasingly dominate the stand, and oak is eventually shaded out. Prior to Euro-American settlement, American Indians who gathered acorns for food frequently burned Oregon white oak woodlands to favor the tree. This killed the young conifers and led to grassy understories. These low-intensity grass fires often caused only minor canopy damage to oaks. Prescribed fire is once again being used in many Pacific Northwest woodlands to control competition from woody vegetation. Understory conditions have changed, however. Where shrubs have replaced grass, fire burns hotter and causes more tree damage.

Because white oak flowers and leaves form inside the buds one year prior to actual flowering, researchers found that buds are particularly vulnerable to summer fire damage. Researchers were able to relate fire intensity to acorn production. Even when tree buds are not killed, flowering and acorn production the following year may be reduced. This information will help land mangers effectively use prescribed burns to manage oak woodlands and wildlife that depend on acorns for food.

Contact: David Peter, dpeter@fs.fed.us, Threat Characterization and Management Program

Partner: U.S. Department of Defense, Joint Base Lewis-McChord

Dave Peter

A prescribed burn in a stand of Oregon white oak will keep fuel levels low and help prevent conifers from encroaching.

Aftermath of 2002 Biscuit Fire, Siskiyou National Forest, Oregon.

Postfire management influences later plant communities

RESTORING BURNED forests on federal lands in southwest Oregon may have multiple objectives, including protecting site productivity, maintaining diversity of species in the near and long term, and developing structurally complex mature stands. Station scientists have monitored various reforestation methods that were applied to burned plantations following the 2002 Timbered Rock Fire. They observed that removing competing vegetation had a greater effect on the composition of plant communities than did planting conifer seedlings.

Woody shrubs were cut back repeatedly during the first 3 years following conifer planting. This did not remove shrubs from the sites, but the temporary reduction in their abundance resulted in the early development of different postfire vegetation communities, when compared to sites where woody shrubs were not cut back. Initial increases in the occurrence of nonnative invasive species were very small, suggesting that the reforestation treatments were not likely to directly lead to invasive species problems.

This information may be useful to land managers in southwest Oregon who are preparing postfire strategies for reforestation, vegetation, and fuel management. It can also be applied more broadly by modelers interested in predicting postfire vegetation and fuel dynamics at stand and landscape scales.

Contact: Paul D. Anderson, pdanderson@fs.fed.us, Land and Watershed Management Program

Partners: Oregon State University, USDI Bureau of Land Management

Forests and Grasslands

Key Findings and Products

▷ New field guide highlights 56 of the most prevalent or problematic nonnative invasive plants in Pacific Coast forests.

▷ Landscape models indicate that sage grouse breeding habitat may historically have been more abundant than current management plans recommend.

▷ Spatial modeling helps land managers locate sudden oak death in Oregon and prioritize eradication efforts.

 Tools

Forest Sector Carbon Calculator Software (FSCC)

Description:
This online tool allows users to compare how stores of carbon in the forest and in forest products change over time following forest harvest and wildfire. The calculator is designed to give users a way to compare the short- and long-term effects of different forest management practices, wildfire occurrence, and assumptions about forest product use. It contains tutorials and produces graphs and data that can be downloaded for further analysis. It is intended to complement more technical models that are used to give precise estimates of actual levels of carbon storage for particular stands or landscapes with good forest inventory information.

Use:
This carbon calculator is designed for forest managers and educators who want to know how forest management practices might affect carbon storage and flux in forests and forest products. The tool will facilitate more informed debates, decisions, and policies concerning carbon and forest management.

How to get it:
http://landcarb.forestry.oregonstate.edu/

Contact:
Tom Spies, tspies@fs.fed.us, Ecological Process and Function Program

Virtual Trail for Olympic Habitat Development Study

Description:
This interactive Web site features photos, maps, and original artwork. Visitors can explore a study site on the Olympic Peninsula and learn about some of the silvicultural techniques that have been suggested for use in accelerating the development of structures and ecological communities associated with old-growth forests.

Use:
Natural resource professionals are using it to learn more about variable-density thinning, an experimental technique being used to accelerate development of old-growth characteristics. It will also be of interest to anyone wanting to learn more about the plants and animals found in conifer forests on the Olympic Peninsula.

How to get it:
http://www.fs.fed.us/pnw/olympia/silv/ohds/

Contact:
Connie Harrington, charrington@fs.fed.us, Land and Watershed Management Program

◁ Coyote Wall, Washington. Photo by Keith Routman.

 Tools

---

Seedlot Selection Tool

Description:
The Seedlot Selection Tool is a GIS mapping program designed to help forest managers match seedlots with planting sites based on climate information. The tool can be used to map current climates, or future climates based on selected climate change scenarios.

Use:
Although the Seedlot Selection Tool is tailored for matching seedlots and planting sites, it can be used by anyone interested in mapping present or future climates defined by temperature and precipitation. Forest geneticists in the Pacific Northwest and the eastern

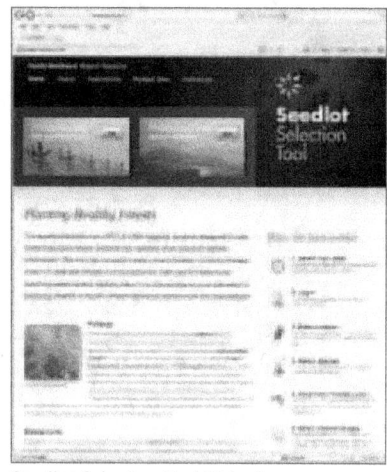
Seedlot Selection Tool Web site.

United States have begun to use this tool to map climates corresponding to specific seed zones of interest, explore the ranges of climates within seed zones, and indicate how the locations of those climates change in the future.

How to get it:
http://sst.forestry.oregonstate.edu/pnw/

Contact:
Brad St. Clair, bstclair@fs.fed.us, Land and Watershed Management Program

Partner:
Oregon State University

Center for Forest Provenance Data

Description:
The Center for Forest Provenance Data is a centralized data and information management system designed to archive data from long-term provenance tests and seedling genecology studies and make those data available to facilitate collaboration among researchers. A provenance test is a planting where population samples from different geographical areas are grown together in one or more locations.

Use:
The Center for Forest Provenance Data promotes national and international collaboration among researchers studying the genetics of adaptation, as well as natural and managed responses to climate change. Over the past century, many provenance studies of forest trees have been established around the world, resulting in considerable long-term field

data and seedling genecological information. These data are invaluable for developing and refining seed transfer guidelines, testing forest growth models, and understanding how trees will respond to climate change, as well as other uses yet to be determined. Researchers have begun to archive data in the database and make it available for collaboration.

How to get it:
http://cenforgen.forestry.oregonstate.edu/index.php

Contact:
Brad St. Clair, bstclair@fs.fed.us, Land and Watershed Management Program

Partner:
Oregon State University

LandTrendr and TimeSync

Description:
These tools are used in tandem to detect trends in forest disturbance and recovery. LandTrendr (Landsat-based detection of Trends in Disturbance and Recovery) is a mapping tool that automatically extracts information on land surface changes (e.g.,

fire, insect and disease damage, timber harvesting or regrowth) from Landsat satellite imagery. TimeSync is a companion image interpretation software tool for synchronizing algorithm and human interpretations of Landsat imagery. These tools capture both short-duration events such as harvest and fire, and long-term trends such as declines in forest health and regrowth. Researchers can use these new tools to comprehensively map change over every Landsat pixel (30 m) since 1972 in forested ecosystems and understand the accuracy of the maps.

Use:

The National Park Service uses these tools for its inventory and monitoring program. The Forest Service Pacific Northwest Region uses them for the Effectiveness Monitoring Program of the Northwest Forest Plan. The PNW Research Station, Oregon State University, NASA Goddard Space Flight Center, and the University of Maryland are using these tools to help characterize the U.S. carbon budget.

How to get it:
http://landtrendr.forestry.oregonstate.edu/
http://www.fsl.orst.edu/larse/

Contact:
Warren Cohen, wcohen@fs.fed.us,
Resource Monitoring and Assessment Program

Partners:
Oregon State University, NASA, University of Maryland, USDA Forest Service Rocky Mountain Research Station

PNW-FIADB

Description:

This tool allows users to work with the database populated and maintained by the Pacific Northwest Research Station's Forest Inventory and Analysis team. Users can answer questions about the status and trends of forest resources by summarizing data on live and dead trees, down woody materials (fuels), and understory vegetation.

Use:

Resource managers and policymakers can use this tool to help inform their decisionmaking process. The LANDFIRE project used the database to update its comprehensive fuels maps and spatial data layers for the Pacific Northwest. The California Climate Action Registry used the database to develop baseline levels of carbon stocks in private forests in the state. The database was used to quickly respond to congressional requests about biomass size distribution and the availability of wood supplies from national forests.

Contact:
Karen Waddell, kwaddell@fs.fed.us,
Resource Monitoring and Assessment Program

Forest Inventory and Analysis crew in Alaska conducts daily briefing.

New field guide highlights nonnative invasive plants found in Pacific Coast forests

NONNATIVE PLANTS affect the composition and function of natural and managed ecosystems. They can limit or degrade land use options and can be costly to eradicate. Despite their influence, very little comprehensive information on the abundance, distribution, and impact of nonnative invasive plants is available. To remedy this, researchers developed a prioritized list of nonnative invasive plants affecting forest lands in the Pacific coastal states of California, Oregon, and Washington. They produced a field guide featuring 56 invasive plants believed to be the most prevalent or problematic. The color photos of each plant in various stages of development and written descriptions in nontechnical language facilitate reliable identification in the field.

The PNW Forest Inventory and Analysis program (FIA) is considering adopting the list and guide for targeted sampling of nonnative plants. Future FIA analyses would be able to assess the distribution and impact of these key nonnative species more effectively than current protocols.

Contact: Andy Gray, agray01@fs.fed.us, Resource Monitoring and Assessment Program

Partners: Institute of Applied Ecology, University of Washington

For more information: Gray, A.N.; Barndt, K.; Reichard, S.H. 2011. Nonnative invasive plants of Pacific coast forests: a field guide for identification. Gen. Tech. Rep. PNW-GTR-817. Portland, OR: U.S. Department of Agriculture, Forest Service, Pacific Northwest Research Station. 91 p. http://www.fs.fed.us/pnw/pubs/pnw_gtr817.pdf

Seeding native grasses on soil with Scotch broom seeds slows development of this invasive species

SCOTCH BROOM (*Cytisus scoparius*) is a large nonnative shrub that has invaded forest and prairie sites throughout western Oregon and Washington. It produces many seeds that remain viable for several years, enabling Scotch broom to occupy sites for decades. Several native grasses of the Pacific Northwest, however, show promise as effective competitors for inhibiting development of Scotch broom seedlings.

In greenhouse experiments, three native perennial grass species were seeded into soils containing Scotch broom seeds. Biomass of Scotch broom seedlings decreased by 72 to 90 percent when grown under grass competition. The most competitive species, spike bentgrass (*Agrostis exarata*), was able to colonize all growing space and deplete soil water rapidly. The least competitive species, western fescue (*Festuca occidentalis*), developed more slowly. When combined with Scotch broom control treatments and seedbed preparation, native grass seeding is a promising approach for restoring invaded areas to native grasslands.

Contact: Tim Harrington, tharrington@fs.fed.us, Threat Characterization and Management Program

Partner: Center for Invasive Plant Management, Bozeman, Montana

Tim Harrington

A greenhouse experiment found that native grasses slowed growth of invasive Scotch broom seedlings.

Richard C. Johnson

At the Central Ferry Research Farm in Washington, a geneticist looks for variation in mountain brome grown from different seed sources.

Seed transfer zones for mountain brome identified

MOUNTAIN BROME (*Bromus carinatus*) is a grass commonly used in restoration efforts. This means that populations are regularly transferred from one place to another. This research addresses questions about how far populations may be moved and still adapt to the new environment.

Use: National forests in northeast Oregon and southwest Washington are using these newly identified seed transfer zones in restoration efforts.

Researchers used common-garden studies at two contrasting test sites to evaluate mountain brome from a range of environments in the Blue Mountains. They found that plant traits varied significantly among populations and were frequently correlated to gradients of precipitation and temperature at source locations. The relationships between traits and climates were used to develop maps of genetic variation in multivariate adaptive traits, which were in turn used to delineate seed transfer zones for mountain brome in the Blue Mountains.

Seed transfer zones for mountain brome are being used by the Malheur, Ochoco, Umatilla, and Wallowa-Whitman National Forests to ensure that plant material used in restoration is adapted to the prevailing environmental conditions.

Contact: Brad St. Clair, bstclair@fs.fed.us, Land and Watershed Management Program

Partners: USDA Agricultural Research Service, National Forest System

Native grasses need time but are part of an effective restoration effort

WORLDWIDE, invasive exotic plants have become one of the most pressing issues of grassland conservation and management. Herbicides are the primary method used to control invasive plants. Working in the Oregon Wenaha Wildlife Area, station scientists evaluated restoration efforts applied to grasslands dominated by the invasive plant, sulfur cinquefoil, 6 years after treatments. They found that combining herbicide use with sowing native grass seed was an effective grassland restoration strategy, when combined with temporary livestock exclusion.

Of the five herbicides they evaluated, picloram best controlled sulfur cinquefoil during the study. However, without the addition of native perennial grass seeds, the sites continued to be dominated by exotic grasses. Seeding with native perennial grasses resulted in a 20-percent decrease in exotic grass cover, although success of was not apparent until 6 years after treatment. Seeding success of grassland restoration projects may appear poor in the first years because of the slow growth of native perennial grass species in the interior West, even though recovery is well underway.

Contact: Catherine Parks, cparks01@fs.fed.us, Threat Characterization and Management Program

Partners: Oregon Department of Fish and Wildlife, Oregon State University, Wallowa Resources

Scientists model cheatgrass invasion and pinyon-juniper woodland encroachment into sagebrush

SAGEBRUSH ecosystems are one of the most imperiled in the United States, and the Great Basin ecoregion is particularly threatened by nonnative, invasive cheatgrass and encroaching pinyon-juniper woodland. Cheatgrass invasion can alter fire cycles, leading to more frequent and intense fires that eventually eliminate sagebrush shrublands. Pinyon-juniper encroachment can lead to soil erosion, altered plant communities, losses in forage production, and high risk of crown fires.

Station scientists developed models to predict the risk of cheatgrass invasion and woodland encroachment across watersheds of the Great Basin. They found that watersheds differ in their spatial patterns of habitat abundance and risk, resulting in different implications for conservation and restoration. In central Oregon, they found that the densities and distribution of juniper trees pose substantial risk to sagebrush. Few of the juniper trees that were growing prior to Euro-American settlement (about 140 years ago) remain, and high densities of juniper seedlings and postsettlement junipers indicate extensive encroachment into sagebrush. This information can guide active restoration through targeted removal of encroaching juniper in sagebrush communities in this region.

Land managers from the U.S. Department of the Interior Bureau of Land Management have used these model projections to quantify potential habitat loss to sagebrush-associated species and to highlight watersheds for potential restoration.

Contact: Mary Rowland, mrowland@fs.fed.us, Ecological Process and Function Program

Partners: USDA Forest Service Remote Sensing Applications Center, Rocky Mountain Research Station, Washington Office Terrestrial Ecology Unit

Mary Rowland

Few large, old juniper remain from the years prior to Euro-American settlement.

Encroaching juniper and exotic grasses threaten shrub steppe in southeast Oregon

MANY THREATS are jeopardizing the shrub steppe of the Columbia Basin, including the spread of invasive species such as cheatgrass and expansion of western juniper into shrub steppe beyond its historical range. Native shrub steppe provides important habitat for many wildlife species and is valued for its biodiversity. Land managers have asked for tools to assess risk of shrub steppe conversion and management

Mary Rowland

Encroaching young juniper threaten to alter sagebrush ecosystems.

options for maintaining native shrub steppe. The Integrated Landscape Assessment Project used a state-and-transition modeling approach to project changes in shrub steppe vegetation over time. Without aggressive management, cheatgrass is expected to increase in many warm, dry Wyoming big sagebrush communities, and juniper invasion is likely to expand throughout much of the cool, moist mountain big sagebrush habitat where seed sources are readily available. In transitional communities between Wyoming big sagebrush and mountain big sagebrush zones, researchers expect much of the landscape to convert to either cheatgrass or juniper woodland.

Contact: Miles Hemstrom, mhemstrom@fs.fed.us, Focused Science Delivery Program

Partners: Institute for Natural Resources, Oregon State University

---

Amount of historical sage grouse habitat differs slightly from current recommendations

SAGEBRUSH ecosystems in the western United States face several threats, including invasive grasses, which lead to different fire regimes, and development. As this habitat has declined, species such as the sage grouse that depend on sagebrush ecosystems have become a management concern. Researchers analyzed how much sage grouse habitat might have existed prior to 1850 and how that amount compares to current management recommendations. By using the Vegetation Dynamics Development Tool, researchers identified reference conditions for the Malheur High Plateau in eastern Oregon and estimated historical breeding, brood-rearing, and wintering habitat. Their models showed that the median amount of sage grouse breeding habitat may have been slightly more abundant than levels currently recommended, but wintering habitat may have been less abundant. These results suggest that either sage grouse do not need as much winter habitat as sage grouse biologists recommend or that the amount of winter habitat may have constrained sage grouse populations.

Contact: Miles Hemstrom, mhemstrom@fs.fed.us, Focused Science Delivery Program

Partners: Oregon State University, USDI Bureau of Land Management

---

Postfire cattle grazing affects ponderosa pine forest understory plants more than reintroduction of fire

PRESCRIBED FIRE is used to manage and restore millions of acres of forests in western North America, and livestock grazing occurs on approximately 91 percent of all federal lands in the West. Yet, few studies have experimentally examined the interaction of prescribed fire and cattle grazing in western interior forests.

To better understand ecosystem response to these combined management regimes, station scientists evaluated grazing effects (grazing, no grazing) on ponderosa pine plant communities over five growing seasons after prescribed fire reburns (spring, fall, no burn). They found that for all treatments (including no burning), excluding cattle grazing for five seasons significantly

Becky Kerns

Researchers examined the effects of prescribed burns and grazing on understory vegetation in a ponderosa pine forest.

increased the total vegetative cover, native perennial forb cover, grass height, grass flowering density, and shrub cover. The 5-year study found that grazing exclusion in this setting caused a greater degree of change in vegetation than the initial reintroduction of fire.

Contact: Becky Kerns, bkerns@fs.fed.us,
Threat Characterization and Management Program

Partner: USDA Forest Service Malheur National Forest

Retaining logging debris on site sustains soil productivity

LOGGING DEBRIS that remains after forest harvesting is currently viewed by some land managers as a hindrance to tree planting, a source of fuels for wildfire, and a potential feedstock for energy, but new research indicates that it provides important ecosystem functions. At two sites in western Oregon and Washington, logging debris was found to act as a mulch to conserve soil water, and the additional water promoted survival and growth of planted Douglas-fir seedlings. On soils low in carbon and nitrogen, retaining logging debris resulted in greater accumulations of these elements after 5 years, compared to areas where debris had been removed. By insulating and cooling the soil surface, the debris reduced losses of soil carbon from microbial respiration or leaching of soluble forms. These

accumulations of soil carbon and nitrogen will help to improve and sustain productivity of forest soils.

Glacial outwash soils of the Puget Sound region are likely to benefit from logging debris retention after forest harvesting because of their droughty, coarse texture and innately small pools of soil carbon and nitrogen.

Contact: Tim Harrington, tharrington@fs.fed.us,
Threat Characterization and Management Program

Partners: Green Diamond Resource Company; Port Blakely Tree Farms, LLC; Virginia Tech; University of Minnesota

Site quality indicators and maximum stand density calculated for western redcedar

WESTERN REDCEDAR is an ecologically and economically important tree species in the Pacific Northwest. Its ability to grow in deep shade makes it as an important component in forest stands with multiple canopy layers. It is a species that most people can identify on sight, but surprisingly little information was available on its growth rates under various stand and management conditions and how environmental variables influence site quality. To remedy this, station scientists compiled data from more than 73,000 trees from several western states and Canadian provinces to look at these relationships. They also examined data from research trials on thinning and fertilization and from a large network of ecology plots. They determined the climate variables most important for site quality of redcedar and calculated maximum stand density index—a parameter in many growth models. They also compared growth rates of western redcedar to Douglas-fir, a common tree associate, under different types of stand conditions.

Use:
Public and private forests use findings to manage western redcedar.

Managers from the Washington Department of Natural Resources, Green Crow, and Starker Forests are using this information to identify areas to plant redcedar and stands that warrant thinning, and to evaluate the projected effects of alternative management scenarios.

Contact: Connie Harrington, charrington@fs.fed.us,
Land and Watershed Management Program

Partners: British Columbia Ministry of Forests, Green Crow, Starker Forests, Washington Department of Natural Resources, USDA Forest Service Pacific Northwest Region

Scientists develop cost-effective method for identifying genetic markers in threatened and endangered conifer species

CONSERVING and managing natural populations requires accurate and inexpensive genotyping methods to identify parentage, movement and migration, estimates of effective population sizes, and rates of inbreeding. Microsatellites are among the most popular genetic markers because they are easy to use, simple to analyze, and clearly identify genetic differences. Microsatellite development has historically been prohibitively expensive, and has been sparingly applied to domesticated species and species of the highest conservation concern. By adapting multiplexed massively parallel sequencing—an approach pioneered by PNW Research Station geneticists—station scientists developed a cost-effective method for identifying thousands of microsatellite markers from any organism. They used this approach to identify more than 1 million genetic markers for 30 conifer and bird species.

Use:
PNW and Alaska Regions use genetic markers in efforts to conserve Port-Orford cedar and yellow-cedar.

These markers are helping to guide *Phytopthora*-resistance breeding in Port-Orford cedar in the Pacific Northwest, and to characterize genetic variation in yellow-cedar in the Alaska Region. Genetic markers are available for threatened whitebark pine and torrey pine, charismatic giant sequoia, and landscape dominants like ponderosa pine. These genetic tools are available without restriction at http://openwetware.org/wiki/Conifermicrosat/.

Contact: Rich Cronn, rcronn@fs.fed.us, Land and Watershed Management Program

Partners: Oregon State University; USDA Forest Service Special Technology and Development Program, Dorena Genetic Resource Center; U.S. Geological Survey

These young Port-Orford cedars are resistant to an introduced root rot fungus (*Phytophthora lateralis*) that has decimated much of the species. Station scientists are working with partners to screen potential clones for genetic resistance to the fungus.

Connie Harrington

Drought-related constraints on Douglas-fir growth are not primarily those of photosynthesis

AS TREES grow, they sequester increasing amounts of atmospheric carbon, and thus have a crucial role in mitigating climate change. Climate projections for many areas of the western United States indicate the likelihood of longer dry spells, which would inhibit tree growth. The exact mechanisms behind drought and decreased tree growth, however, are not known.

To better understand this, researchers analyzed shoot growth, plant and soil water stress, and storage of nonstructural carbohydrates in stem wood, branch tips, and foliage of Douglas-fir across a range of tree heights over 17 months. They found that contrary to previously accepted hypotheses, increasing drought severity leads to scenarios in which photosynthesis is less a determinant of productivity than other factors such as cell expansion and long-distance transport of carbon within trees.

Findings from this study can be used to improve models in which tree growth is primarily determined by the degree to which parameters such as humidity, soil moisture, and temperature limit a tree's ability to obtain carbon via photosynthesis. This may improve our understanding of how current and future climates may influence forest productivity.

Contact: David Woodruff, dwoodruff@fs.fed.us, Ecological Process and Function Program

Greater demand for bioenergy could lead to less forest land, more cropland in Midwest

LAND USE in the United States is influenced by many economic and social factors. One of the most important recent influences on land use in the United States has been the increasing use of corn-based ethanol in bioenergy production. High energy prices have sparked substantial growth in ethanol production and demand for corn, which could lead to loss of forests as landowners shift to agricultural uses.

Station scientists explored the relationship between land use and aesthetic or environmental values for forest land in Ohio, Indiana, and Illinois. Results suggest that as population density increases, desire for aesthetic amenities associated with open space or recreation could potentially lead to more forest land, relative to cropland. With a higher emphasis on bioenergy, however, a dramatically different future is presented, in which large areas of forest land are lost in the next 40 years.

Contact: Ralph Alig, ralig@fs.fed.us, Goods, Services, and Values Program

Tom Iraci

Maybeso Experimental Forest, Alaska.

Initial reduction in carbon pools following fuel treatment is likely temporary

STATION SCIENTISTS applied species-specific regional equations for tree volume and aboveground live tree biomass estimations to a landscape in central Oregon. They demonstrated how outputs from vegetation simulation models can be used for a variety of landscape analyses, including timber products, biomass supply, and carbon accounting under an active fuel treatment management scenario.

The simulations suggest that an active fuel-treatment management approach might initially reduce the amount of carbon stored in trees. After the first 50 years of the 300-year simulation, aboveground carbon pools in forests less susceptible to severe wildfire or insect outbreaks were increasing steadily and approaching what they had been prior to fuel treatments.

Contact: Xiaoping Zhou, xzhou@fs.fed.us, Focused Science Delivery Program

---

With sufficient incentive, Alaska forests could be managed to store carbon

THE ENVIRONMENTAL Protection Agency is considering mechanisms to control the emission of greenhouse gases, which pose a threat to the environment and public health. One regulatory tool being considered is a cap and trade system, in which a ceiling is set for allowable carbon dioxide emissions, and forest management activities that increase carbon sequestration or reduce use of fossil fuels can be assigned a dollar value and sold to an emitting organization. With Alaska's vast forests, which account for 17 percent of all forest land in the United States, this type of system could have a substantial impact here. Station scientists developed a report that addresses the basic principles of a cap and trade system and its potential impact on Alaska's forest stakeholders. However, because Alaska forest landowners would face high operating costs for afforestation and reforestation projects, the price of carbon offsets would have to be high enough to cover these costs and provide a reasonable return on investment.

Contact: Allen Brackley, abrackley@fs.fed.us, Goods, Services, and Values Program

Partners: University of Alaska Fairbanks, University of Washington

The power of models will transmute this diameter measurement into an estimate of live carbon mass (the sum of stem, branches, bark, and roots) for this tree, which will be expanded several thousand-fold to account for all the trees in the forested landscape that this sample tree represents.

Choice of model influences live-tree carbon estimates

ESTIMATES of the amount of carbon stored in a tree are influenced by numerous uncertainties. One of them is model-selection uncertainty: the user has to choose among multiple empirical equations and conversion factors that can be plausibly justified as locally applicable to calculate the carbon store from inventory measurements such as tree height and diameter at breast height. Researchers quantified model-selection uncertainty for the five most common tree species in northwest Oregon. They found that model-selection error may introduce 20 to 40 percent uncertainty into a live-tree carbon estimate, making this form of error the largest source of uncertainty when estimating live-tree carbon stores. Uncertainty from sampling error, represented as a 95-percent confidence interval, was only 6 percent. Predicted carbon content of individual trees can vary even more among model aggregating pathways, especially the predictions for large trees, which on the Pacific Coast comprise an unusually large share of carbon stores.

Model-selection uncertainty is not an easily remedied error and may call into question the premise of tracking forest carbon with the precision and accuracy required to support contemplated offset protocols. The greatest risk is the potential for choosing a particular calculation pathway to justify a preferred outcome.

Contact: Jeremy Fried, jsfried@fs.fed.us, Resource Monitoring and Assessment Program

Partner: Oregon State University

Knot detection improves with nondestructive method for assessing wood quality

KNOTS and other defects in wood products come in a variety of sizes, shapes, types, and colors. When products are visually inspected, it can be difficult to accurately assess the effects of these defects on wood quality. Researchers found that acoustic technology tools are simple to use and a relatively inexpensive way to test wood quality. They took acoustic velocity measurements of

Dean Perry

A technician marks veneer sheets to determine if wood-product properties can be predicted from acoustically tested tree properties.

Douglas-fir trees in Oregon and Washington using hand-held sensors. Veneer sheets were subsequently peeled from felled trees, and were then digitally analyzed for wood quality characteristics. The researchers found that the digital knot detection technique was accurate and can be used to create digital log models. They are continuing to use acoustic measurement to investigate the relationship between the average stiffness of veneer sheets, stiffness of the log, and stiffness of the parent tree from a range of silvicultural treatments. This technology has the potential to add value all along the forest-to-products chain.

Contact: Eini Lowell, elowell@fs.fed.us, Goods, Services, and Values Program

Partners: Scion Research

Updated log-to-lumber conversion rates reflect improved utilization of small logs

Over the past 40 years, sawmills in the western United States have become more efficient. They now produce more lumber while using less timber. This efficiency occurred even as the size of logs used by sawmills decreased. This finding, based on a review of forest industry surveys, meant the primary technique for estimating lumber production based on volume of harvest wood was now outdated. The Scribner Log Rule was developed in 1846 and was designed to estimate board foot volume that could be produced from a log. As the

USDA Forest Service

Because mills use small logs more efficiently than in the past, log-to-lumber conversion rates needed to be updated.

wood-processing industry has diversified to produce not only lumber but pulp, composite panels, and wood-based fuels, the industry needs to be able to accurately estimate the volume of wood fiber available for use.

Thus, scientists updated conversion rates and recovery factors that are essential for estimating production efficiency, timber supply and demand, and whole-tree volume, which is required for biomass assessments and carbon accounting.

Contact: Jean Daniels, jdaniels@fs.fed.us, Goods, Services, and Values Program

Partners: University of Montana, Western Washington University

Forest Inventory and Analysis in the Pacific Islands

RESEARCHERS collected, analyzed, and summarized field data gathered on islands throughout the western Pacific. They summarized forest information for the Federated States of Micronesia and compared it to prior vegetation mapping work done there. Researchers found that the extreme diversity of vegetation across Micronesia can be attributed to differences in longitudinal climatic influences and human land use practices. Similar data collection and analysis of forest resources were done on the Commonwealth of the Northern Mariana Islands; there researchers found that urban areas have grown, contributing to losses in forest land area. On the Marshall Islands, rising sea level is threatening numerous native plant species.

Data and summaries from these inventories are used by island groups to develop their statewide assessments and resource strategies that enable them to compete for funding. The data also are used to guide resource management and policy decisions.

Contact: Joseph Donnegan, jdonnegan@fs.fed.us, Resource Monitoring and Assessment Program

Partners: American Samoa Forestry; Department of Land and Natural Resources, Commonwealth of the Northern Mariana Islands; Federated States of Micronesia Forestry; Kosrae Forestry; Marshall Islands Forestry; National Tropical Botanical Garden; University of Guam; USDA Forest Service Pacific Southwest Research Station Region, State and Private Forestry

Mika Falaniko

Field crew work around tidal fluctuations as they inventory forest conditions in a mangrove swamp on the island of Kosrae in the Federated States of Micronesia.

Collaboration explores an ecosystem services stewardship approach on national forests

THE PNW Research Station is collaborating with the Deschutes National Forest to explore how an ecosystem services approach could be used to organize and enhance forest stewardship activities in central Oregon. Current natural resource agency accounting systems define management accomplishments in terms of output-oriented program targets, such as board feet of timber sold or acres treated to reduce fire risk. These metrics describe actions undertaken, but do not account for the non-market goods and services provided by public lands. This project provides examples of how management activities and performance measures could be characterized in terms of ecosystem services.

This project aims to apply an operational ecosystem service approach in a forest management context. It uses the Deschutes National Forest as a place-based model showing how ecosystem services could be used as a framework for enhancing forest stewardship. It is demonstrating the possibilities of this approach in a way relevant to managers and policymakers.

Contact: Robert Deal, rdeal@fs.fed.us,
Goods, Services, and Values Program

Partners: Defenders of Wildlife, Willamette Partnership, USDA Forest Service Deschutes National Forest

Airborne laser data combined with field surveys facilitates landscape planning

FORESTERS RELY on inventory data to understand the condition and distribution of the trees they manage. Traditionally, this information came from stand exams, which can be labor-intensive and difficult to obtain for landscape-scale management decisions. This study, conducted on the Malheur National Forest in eastern Oregon, found that Light Detection and Ranging (LIDAR) data, in combination with field plots, generated a stand-level forest inventory of structural attributes comparable to one produced from stand exams. By exploring the potential of remote sensing technologies to provide landscape-scale data, this study helps forest science stay current with the evolving needs of forest managers. In turn, landscape-scale data can support a variety of research objectives, which can facilitate the integration of disciplines and enhance collaborative landscape planning and assessments.

Use: Malheur National Forest uses data to select stands for fuel reduction treatments.

Malheur National Forest staff helped design and implement this study, and are using the results to weigh the cost-effectiveness of traditional forest inventory versus satellite and LIDAR-derived

Scott Lake, Deschutes National Forest, Oregon.

Jim Hughes

James Dollins

Oregon white oak stand.

estimates of forest structure. They are also using the data to identify target stands for fuel-reduction treatments. Study results are also being used in the National Enhanced Elevation Assessment, which is sponsored by the National Digital Elevation Program and includes the Forest Service, other agencies, and nongovernmental organizations.

Contact: Susan Hummel, shummel@fs.fed.us, Goods, Services, and Values Program

Partners: Malheur National Forest; Michigan Technological University; USDA Remote Sensing Applications Center, Rocky Mountain Research Station

Dave Peter

Oregon white oak acorns.

New models help detect spread of sudden oak death

SUDDEN OAK death (SOD) was discovered in Oregon forests in 2001. Despite considerable control efforts, the disease continues to spread. In response, scientists developed two models to map where SOD was likely to become established and its risk of spread. The scientists determined that 40 square miles of forested land were likely invaded by 2009, and that the disease threatens more than 1,300 square miles of forests across western Oregon. The greatest risk is in southwest Oregon where susceptible host species, such as tanoak, are concentrated. The Oregon Department of Forestry and other agencies are using the models to prioritize early detection and eradication efforts in the state.

Use: Oregon Department of Forestry uses models in eradication efforts.

Contact: Janet Ohmann, johmann@fs.fed.us, Resource Monitoring and Assessment Program

Partners: Oregon Department of Forestry, Oregon State University, University of North Carolina at Charlotte

Watershed Health

Key Findings and Products

▷ The number of Chinook salmon and the size of steelhead trout increased in areas where in-stream habitat restoration efforts occurred in the upper Columbia River basin.

▷ Long-term trends in temperature of western North American streams show both cooling and warming trends.

▷ Everyday effects of vegetation on soil carbon loss may be as important as wildfire to carbon budgets.

 **Tools**

Riparian Management Explorer

Description:
This tool is used to explore the implications of different riparian management options for future wood recruitment and abundance of in-stream wood. The Riparian Management Explorer illustrates how differences in riparian-management buffer widths and thinning prescriptions within each buffer affect expected recruitment rates and abundance of large wood.

The tool is flexible, accommodating different stand-growth models, topography, bole-taper equations, and bank erosion rates. Results, using either wood volume or number of pieces, can be viewed graphically for (1) recruitment rate and in-stream abundance over time, or (2) the amount of wood accumulated as a function of distance from the channel edge at a specific future date. Results can be formulated in terms of wood-piece diameter, the diameter of the source trees, and by source-tree species classes (hardwood or conifer).

Use:
Riparian Management Explorer was designed specifically for the U.S. Forest Service and the National Oceanic and Atmospheric Administration to aid in discussions of riparian management options and potential effects on future fish habitat. It may be used by public and private forest managers to explore the effects of riparian management alternatives.

How to get it:
http://www.netmaptools.org/

Contact:
Gordon Reeves, greeves@fs.fed.us,
Land and Watershed Management Program

◁ Stream in the Columbia Gorge, Oregon.
Photo © by Miles Hemstrom.

A GIS-based tool for linking field and digital stream data

Description:
This tool based on a geographic information system (GIS) matches stream-survey data to digitally produced stream layers created with NetStream software. The output is a shapefile of survey reaches with both the survey data and attributes associated with the digitally produced stream layer (e.g., drainage area, gradient, and valley width). It enables users to extrapolate survey results to unsurveyed streams by using GIS to estimate habitat abundance, potential fish abundance, or fish carrying capacity, for example.

Use:
This tool was collaboratively funded and is being used by the U.S. Forest Service, Kalispel Tribe, Oregon Watershed Enhancement Board, and Arctic Yukon Kuskokwim Sustainable Salmon Initiative.

How to get it:
http://www.netmaptools.org/

Contact:
Kelly Burnett, kmburnett@fs.fed.us,
Land and Watershed Management Program

Aquatic and riparian state and transition models for the Blue Mountains of northeastern Oregon and the northern Oregon Coast Range

Description:
These state and transition models simulate the effects of plant succession, natural disturbance, land use and restoration practices on conditions of riparian forests, channel morphology, and salmon habitat. State classes in the models are defined by channel morphology and riparian vegetation. Transitions are defined by plant succession, natural disturbances (floods, debris flows, wildfires, native ungulate browsing), land use activities (fuel treatments, timber harvests, livestock grazing) and restoration practices (planting riparian hardwoods, exclusion of domestic livestock or native ungulate browsing). Habitat suitability rankings for anadromous salmonids (migration, spawning, winter rearing, summer rearing) are derived from channel and vegetation attributes associated with each state in the models.

The models were specifically designed for two watersheds: the upper Middle Fork John Day River in the interior Columbia River basin and the Wilson River in the Oregon Coast Range. The model structure and the suite of factors simulated in the models are designed for portability so that these models should be reasonably easy to modify and apply to other areas in the Blue Mountains or Coast Range. Further, the models will serve as a template for developing new models for more distant regions.

Use:
The models are designed for landscape planners.

How to get it:
http://www.fs.fed.us/pnw/lwm/aem/projects/ar_models.html

Contact:
Steve Wondzell, swondzell@fs.fed.us,
Land and Watershed Management Program

Global Bd Mapping Project database

Description:
Batrachochytrium dendrobatidis (Bd) is a disease-causing fungus that is devastating amphibian populations worldwide. This Web-based mapping project facilitates communication between scientists and natural resource managers as they try to learn more about the fungus and assess risk to local amphibian populations.

Use:
Scientists and managers use the Web site to determine locations of Bd worldwide. Scientists have used this information to determine where to conduct surveillance for Bd or learn who to contact for information from an area. Managers use this information to assess risk to populations and make strategic decisions about reintroducing amphibian species or conducting surveillance or disinfection activities. In 2011, the database was updated with more than 2,000 new records.

How to get it: http://www.Bd-maps.net/

Contact:
Dede Olson, dedeolson@fs.fed.us,
Land and Watershed Management Program

Partners:
Imperial College, London, United Kingdom;
Partners in Amphibian and Reptile Conservation

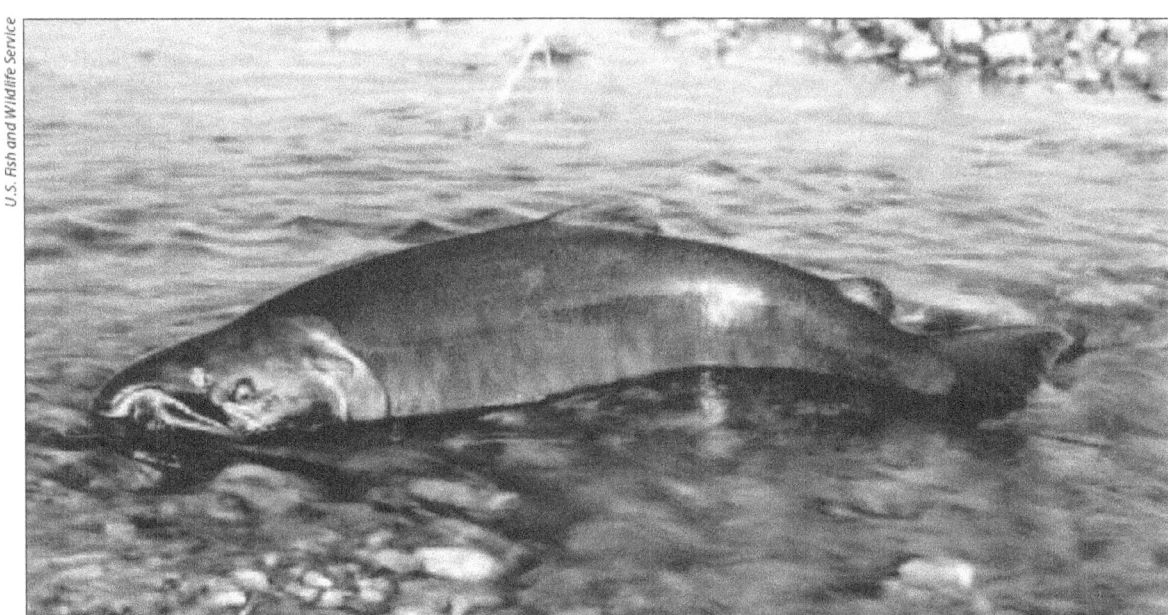

U.S. Fish and Wildlife Service

Chinook salmon.

In-stream restoration efforts benefit Chinook salmon and steelhead trout

STATION SCIENTISTS and cooperators evaluated the effectiveness of in-stream habitat restoration structures designed to enhance rearing habitat for juvenile salmonids. Habitat restoration structures consisted of engineered logjams and rock barbs extending from streambanks in the Entiat River watershed of the upper Columbia River basin. The researchers found that the number of juvenile fish from a threatened run of Chinook salmon were greater in microhabitats with restoration structures compared to microhabitats without the structures. Steelhead trout, although less abundant in restored microhabitats, possibly because of competition from Chinook salmon, showed faster growth rates compared to steelhead trout in untreated microhabitats.

The information is being used by restoration planners and by a larger monitoring program to further inform the design and implementation of additional restoration structures in the same watershed and in other watersheds throughout the upper Columbia River basin.

Contact: Karl Polivka, kpolivka@fs.fed.us, Land and Watershed Management Program

Partners: Bonneville Power Administration; Cascadia Conservation District; National Marine Fisheries Service, Integrated Status and Effectiveness Monitoring Program

Scientists develop sampling and modeling tools to characterize microclimates in riparian areas

PROVIDING high-quality habitat for fish, amphibians, and other aquatic and riparian organisms is one management objective for headwater forests in the Pacific Northwest. The compatibility of timber harvest or other vegetation manipulations with quality riparian and aquatic habitat is often contingent on the effects these disturbances may have on riparian microclimate. Microclimate changes with distance from the streams. The ability to predict this variation and the influences of upslope harvesting and riparian buffers is important when designing management and monitoring strategies that will provide quality aquatic and riparian habitats while affording opportunities for the production of wood and other ecosystem services.

Microclimate data can be difficult and expensive to collect, so in this study, efficient sampling strategies were developed to account for the spatial variation in riparian forest structure and its influence on microclimate. Understory air temperature was then modeled based on topographic and forest structure. With increasing availability of remotely sensed forest structure data, this type of modeling may prove an efficient way to indirectly monitor microclimate attributes and to incorporate those attributes into forest management planning tools.

The modeling efforts have yielded insights to the relative accuracy and bias of alternative modeling approaches. Near-term utility is emerging in discussions among land managers and regulatory entities about the width of riparian buffers needed to mitigate potential effects of upslope harvest on the warming of air near streams and stream temperatures.

Contact: Paul D. Anderson, pdanderson@fs.fed.us, Land and Watershed Management Program

Partners: Oregon State University, USDI Bureau of Land Management, U.S. Geological Survey

Alternative buffer designs influence abundance of small mammals along headwater streams

UNDER THE Northwest Forest Plan, all streams on federal land are protected by buffer zones intended to protect riparian and stream ecosystems from logging effects and other human disturbances. Different rules apply to state and private land, however. In Washington state, headwater streams in state and private industrial forests generally are less protected than those on federal land. This discrepancy has led to debate over how much protection fishless headwater streams should receive during logging. To find middle ground, station scientists worked with the Washington Department of Natural Resources (DNR) to evaluate alternative buffering strategies.

The scientists found that several small mammal species responded differently to different buffer widths following logging. The northwestern deer mouse declined in all treatments compared to unlogged drainages, while more creeping vole, southern red-backed vole, and Townsend's chipmunk were found after logging in all buffer treatments. Relative to the unlogged drainages, the overall diversity and total abundance of small mammals did not change significantly following logging in any of the treatments.

These findings support the development of a long-term headwater stream conservation strategy for the DNR and the proposed adaptive management strategy for western Washington.

Contact: Martin Raphael, mrapahel@fs.fed.us, and Randall Wilk, rwilk@fs.fed.us, Ecological Process and Function Program

Partner: Washington State Department of Natural Resources

Martin Raphael

A fixed-width riparian buffer zone with upland timber harvest.

Practical management actions can minimize the effects of climate change on amphibians

LEADING the world campaign to develop practical tools to guard species from the adverse effects of climate change, an ad hoc group of international amphibian experts have compiled innovative examples of habitat protection and mitigation to preserve amphibian species across habitats in several nations. These examples fall into three categories: installation of microclimate and microhabitat refugia, enhancement of breeding sites, and manipulation of water or hydroperiods. Water and temperature

Sally Nickelson

In Seattle's Cedar River Municipal Watershed, managers are placing logs perpendicular to pond shorelines to provide sheltered routes for young frogs leaving the water to disperse across the land.

management approaches are critical for this taxon. Microclimate mitigation tools include creating riparian buffers, restoring stream and pond habitat, and managing for down wood. The group's products aim to bridge science and management, resulting in "adaptation management" approaches for amphibians and climate change.

Research and management agencies around the world are using these practical conservation ideas to take action. To share this information widely, the group maintains a Web page that includes a showcase of innovations and a list of new programs for conserving the rarest species.

For more information:

http://parcplace.org/news-a-events.html

http://www.fs.fed.us/pnw/lwm/aem/news/climate_change_and_herpetofauna.html

Contact: Dede Olson, dedeolson@fs.fed.us, Land and Watershed Management Program

Partners: Department of Climate Change, Canberra ACT, Australia; James Cook University of North Queensland, Australia; University of Queensland, Australia; Griffith University, Gold Coast Campus, Australia; The University of Newcastle, Australia; University of Kent, Canterbury, United Kingdom; Universidade do Estado do Rio de Janeiro, Brazil; University of Helsinki, Finland; Pontificia Universidad Católica del Ecuador; University of Otago, New Zealand; EcoGecko Consultants, New Zealand; Florida International University; University of Washington; U.S. Geological Survey; Aldo Leopold Wilderness Research Institute

Stream gravel bars can be a nitrate source or sink depending on time it takes for water to move through them

EXCESS NITROGEN stemming from human activities is a common water pollutant. Fertilizer runoff, sewage, and fossil fuel emissions all contain nitrogen that often ends up in streams. But aquatic systems are natural filters, able to process and remove some nitrogen. Fully understanding the denitrification process will help efforts to improve water quality.

Station scientists used a stable isotope tracer to track the movement and transformation of nitrate nitrogen in stream water flowing through a 14-foot gravel bar of an upland agricultural stream in the Willamette Valley, Oregon. Dissolved organic carbon and oxygen were used up quickly by microorganisms where stream water entered the head of the gravel bar, leading to initial increases in nitrate and ammonia concentrations. Further into the gravel bar, where travel times exceeded 7 hours, the

Portland General Electric

Gravel bars can influence water temperature and water quality. Clackamas River, Oregon.

scientists observed a net loss of nitrate to denitrification. This suggests that gravel bars could be net sources of nitrate to streams wherever travel times were short, but with longer travel times, denitrification will make gravel bars net sinks of nitrate to streams.

This study provides detailed understanding of the processes that control water quality, especially the processes that remove nitrate from nitrogen-polluted streams.

Contact: Steve Wondzell, swondzell@fs.fed.us, Land and Watershed Management Program

Partner: Oregon State University

Hillslope hydrologic connectivity controls riparian groundwater turnover

HYDROLOGIC connectivity between uplands and near-stream riparian zones is essential for the export of water, nutrients, and other solutes from watersheds. However, our current understanding of the role of riparian zones in buffering watershed-scale export of water and solutes is limited. To learn more about these processes, station scientists and collaborators compared the turnover time for shallow groundwater in riparian areas along four well transects in the Tenderfoot Creek Experimental Forest, Montana. They found that where hillslopes were large and riparian areas were small, hillslope water flowed through the riparian zone so that hillslope and riparian zone water were chemically similar. Conversely, where riparian zones were large relative to the size of the adjacent hillslope, water in the riparian zone was chemically distinct from hillslope-source water. These observations suggest that the relative sizes and spatial arrangement of hillslopes and riparian zones along a stream network is a primary control on the export of water and solutes from watersheds.

This export versus retention of solutes is critically important to stream ecosystem processes determining attributes such as ecosystem productivity and the ability of riparian zones to buffer streams from inputs that could alter water quality.

Contact: Steve Wondzell, swondzell@fs.fed.us, Land and Watershed Management Program

Partners: Montana State University, Pennsylvania State University, U.S. Geological Survey

© Miles Hemstrom

Sandy River, Oregon.

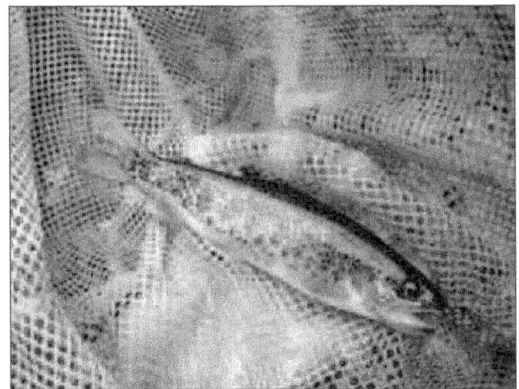

Pete Bisson

Juvenile cutthroat trout.

Novel modeling effort links land use, disturbance, and riparian and aquatic habitats across large landscapes

INTERACTIONS between land use and ecosystem change are complex, especially in riparian zones. To date, few models are available to project the influence of alternative land use practices, natural disturbance, and plant succession on the likely future conditions of riparian zones and aquatic habitats across large landscapes.

Station researchers used a state-and-transition framework to model the effects of various management and restoration practices on conditions of riparian forests, channel morphology, and salmonid habitat. These models incorporate the effects of plant succession, natural disturbances such as fire or native ungulate browsing, management, and restoration practices. Researchers used the models to analyze habitat suitability rankings for two watersheds: the upper Middle Fork John Day River and the Wilson River, Oregon. They found that efforts to improve habitat for anadromous fish in the Middle Fork John Day Basin will likely require considerable work on in-stream conditions, not just management of the adjacent terrestrial and riparian vegetation.

Contact: Steve Wondzell, swondzell@fs.fed.us, Land and Watershed Management Program; Miles Hemstrom, mhemstrom@fs.fed.us, Focused Science Delivery Program

Decision-support systems developed to assess vulnerability and impacts of sulfur deposition across southern Appalachia

THE ENVIRONMENTAL Protection Agency (EPA) and federal land management agencies are concerned with the health of aquatic ecosystems in the southern Appalachian Mountains. Acid rain and dry acidic deposition has increased the sulfate concentration in many Appalachian streams. Coal-fired electric generating facilities, cars, and factories are the main sources of human-caused sulfur emissions.

A large water-sampling network was built in the region over the last few decades, but locations of sampling sites historically were highly biased toward watersheds with high sulfur depositions. Station scientists worked to develop statistical methods that overcame sampling biases and allowed accurate predictions of spatial variables required to assess vulnerability of ecosystems and aquatic biota to atmospheric sulfur deposition across the region. Their results were used to develop a decision-support system of immediate practical value to regional land managers, regulators, and policymakers with the Forest Service, National Park Service, and EPA.

A second decision-support system was developed to predict ecological and biotic impacts of atmospheric sulfur deposition across the southern Appalachian region. It can be used to prioritize watersheds for restoration and protection activities.

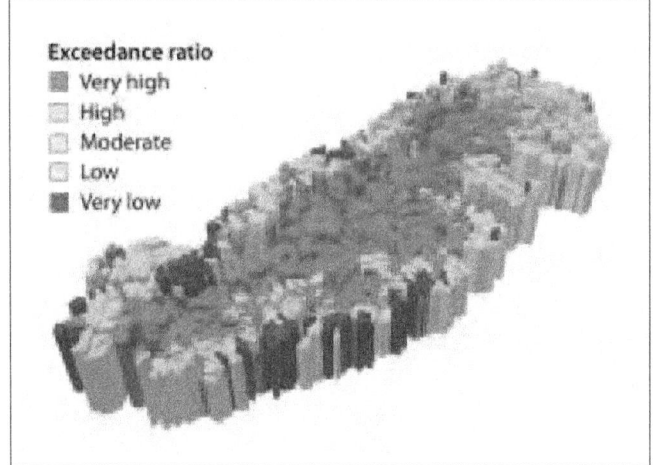

Exceedance ratio
- Very high
- High
- Moderate
- Low
- Very low

Decision support interprets long-term ecosystem effects of atmospheric sulfur deposition in the southern Appalachian region.

Policymakers in the region can use the same system to explore the biological and ecosystem implications of alternative sulfur emission scenarios.

Contact: Paul Hessburg, phessburg@fs.fed.us, and Keith Reynolds, kreynolds@fs.fed.us, Ecological Process and Function Program

Partners: E&S Environmental Services, Environmental Protection Agency, University of Virginia, USDA Forest Service Southern Region

---

Connections between air and stream temperature more complex than previously thought

RECENT WARMING of the terrestrial climate in most parts of the world has motivated concern about corresponding increases in water temperature. Based on observed climate trends in the Pacific Northwest, scientists expected to find warmer streams and increasing temperature variability over time. However, they found as many cooling as warming trends in 18 reference streams across western North America. Winter minimums have been increasing, but summer maximums less so. Scientists compared the reference streams with 45 streams that have been more influenced by humans. The temperatures during the past two decades show mostly cooling trends in minimally human-influenced sites, whereas more human-influenced systems showed mixed responses. The scientists also noted a lack of coherence between air temperature, stream temperature, and flow, which may be related to complex and lagged interactions among nonclimate and climate variables. These findings inform climate researchers as well as state and federal resource managers about temporal trends in stream temperature dynamics.

Contact: Sherri Johnson, sherrijohnson@fs.fed.us, Ecological Process and Function Program

Partners: Oregon State University, U.S. Geological Survey Forest and Rangeland Ecosystem Science Center

Pete Bisson

Thomas Lake, Indian Heaven Wilderness, Gifford Pinchot National Forest.

Field crew learn how to conduct postfire soil surveys.

Soil respiration may influence carbon budgets as much as wildfire

FIRE INTENSITY influences how much soil carbon is released into the atmosphere. Researchers found that intense wildfire associated with high tree mortality induced losses of soil carbon about twice that of lower intensity wildfire and fires set as a backburn. Prescribed fire resulted in about half as much lost soil carbon when compared to intense and moderate wildfire.

In unburned Douglas-fir plantations, however, carbon lost over 11 years through soil respiration had an extrapolated rate equivalent to an intense wildfire every 30 years, suggesting that day-in, day-out vegetation effects on soil carbon are potentially as or more important than wildfire. Soil respiration is a key measurement in the carbon budget.

Researchers have used this data to develop a conceptual model of effects of management on carbon stocks. This model also points out that shrubs have greater potential to increase soil carbon when leaf areas are similar to trees because shrubs have less capability to store carbon above ground.

Improved understanding of the effects of natural disturbance and forest management on carbon budgets will allow land managers to refine estimates of a forest's potential to mitigate climate change.

Contact: Bernard Bormann, bbormann@fs.fed.us, Land and Watershed Management Program

Partners: Oregon State University; Washington Department of Natural Resources Olympic Experimental State Forest; Western Washington State University; USDA Forest Service Rogue River–Siskiyou National Forest, Siuslaw National Forest, Willamette National Forest; USDA Forest Service Pacific Northwest Region Regional Climate Change Program, Regional Ecology Program, Regional Soils Program

Wildlife

Key Findings and Products

▷ West-side nutrition and resource selection models for elk are developed, validated, and used in local habitat evaluation and land management planning in western Oregon and Washington.

▷ Climate change is predicted to shift wolverine distributions, habitat connectivity and dispersal corridors.

▷ Scientists map habitat connectivity, landscape integrity, and climate gradient patterns for 16 wildlife species in Washington.

 **Tools**

Equations for Evaluating Nutritional Quality of Available Moose Forage

Description:
These equations for evaluating the nutritional quality of moose forages are based on laboratory analyses of small quantities of forage samples. Prior to their development, predictive equations for quantifying the nutritional quality of wild, native forages for moose in their natural habitats did not exist.

Use:
Wildlife scientists and land managers can use these equations to quantitatively evaluate habitat for moose anywhere in the world.

How to get it:
Spalinger, D.E.; Collins, W.B.; Hanley, T.A.; Cassara, N.E.; Carnahan, A.M. 2010. The impact of tannins on protein, dry matter, and energy digestion in moose (*Alces alces*). Canadian Journal of Zoology. 88: 977–987.

Contact:
Tom Hanley, thanley@fs.fed.us, Ecological Process and Function Program

New Model Predicts Marten Age Based on Genetic Material

Description:
Researchers developed a Bayesian network model for predicting the age of martens based on chromosomal evidence and other environmental factors. This is the first model of its kind—calibrated and tested with empirical data—that can accurately predict a marten's age by using hair samples or other genetic material collected without actually trapping the animal.

Use:
Researchers can now estimate the population structure (number of animals by age class) solely from indirect evidence such as hair samples, rather than needing to trap and mark or biopsy individual animals. With further testing, such an approach could revolutionize wildlife field research of mammals.

How to get it:
Pauli, J.N.; Whiteman, J.P.; Marcot, B.G. [et al.]. 2011. DNA-based approach to aging martens (*Martes americana* and *M. caurina*). Journal of Mammalogy. 92(3): 500–510.

Contact:
Bruce Marcot, bmarcot@fs.fed.us, Ecological Process and Function Program

Tools

Framework Facilitates Designing Effective Wildlife Corridors

Description:

Wildlife populations in fragmented landscapes experience reduced gene flow, lose genetic diversity over time, and ultimately face greater extinction risk. Improving connectivity in fragmented landscapes is a major focus of conservation biology. Designing effective wildlife corridors for this purpose requires understanding of how landscapes shape gene flow.

Station scientists developed a framework that uses expert opinion as a starting point and then systematically either validates the assumptions of expert opinion or identifies a peak of support for a new model more highly related to genetic isolation. This approach also accounts for interactions between variables, allows for nonlinear responses, and excludes variables that reduce model performance. Station scientists demonstrated its utility on a population of mountain goats inhabiting a fragmented landscape in the Cascade Range, Washington.

Wildlife planners with the Washington Department of Transportation are using this tool to assess landscape connectivity along the I-90 freeway in Washington.

How to get it:
Andrew Shirk, ashirk@fs.fed.us,
Ecological Process and Function Program

New models aid management of elk habitat

ELK ARE widely distributed across western Oregon and Washington, and elk hunting and viewing contribute substantially to rural economies. Elk habitat models and management guidelines had become outdated, so station scientists updated elk nutrition and habitat selection models with an innovative approach that incorporates the latest research on elk nutrition and current spatial

Use:
Tribe, state, and federal land managers use model to manage elk habitat.

data. They used elk radiotelemetry data from many sources and geographic areas to develop and validate these models. They also created maps of nutritional adequacy for elk to evaluate how public access and other factors limit the degree to which nutritional resources are available to elk.

Modeling results are being used to coordinate management of elk habitat and populations among state and federal agencies, Indian tribes, hunting organizations, and other interested groups. The station hosted a workshop for users where several beta testers, including biologists with the Muckleshoot Indian Tribe, Oregon Bureau of Land Management, and Forest Service Pacific Northwest Region, demonstrated how they are incorporating modeling results in local habitat evaluation and land management planning.

Contact: Mary Rowland, mrowland@fs.fed.us, Ecological Process and Function Program

Partners: Boone and Crockett Club, Lower Elwha Klallam Tribe, Makah Nation, Muckleshoot Indian Tribe, National Council for Air and Stream Improvement, National Fish and Wildlife Foundation, Oregon State University, Oregon Department of Fish and Wildlife, Quileute Tribe, Rocky Mountain Elk Foundation, Sauk-Suiattle Indian Tribe, Sporting Conservation Council, USDA Forest Service Pacific Northwest Region, USDI Bureau of Land Management, Washington Department of Fish and Wildlife, West, Inc.

Rachel Cook

Elk calf.

Columbian white-tailed deer avoid livestock areas as fawning habitat

COLUMBIAN white-tailed deer historically ranged throughout much of western Oregon and southwestern Washington. The deer prefer oak woodlands and savannas, ecosystems that have greatly declined since Euro-American settlement. Today, two remnant populations of the deer remain: one lives along the lower Columbia River and the second lives in the interior valleys of the Umpqua Basin in Douglas County, Oregon.

The lower Columbia River population has been federally listed as an endangered species since 1967. The Douglas County population has been protected by the state of Oregon since 1978 and is considered a discrete population with separate recovery goals. The minimum recovery goals have been met, but

White-tailed deer.

the deer occupies less than 5 percent of its historical range. Understanding how land use affects its fawning habitat is fundamental to supporting further recovery of the species.

Scientists found that the does avoided areas with livestock during fawning and chose to give birth in areas concealed by dense vegetation, typically along a permanent stream. Areas with livestock offered less vegetative cover.

Contact: Martin Raphael, mraphael@fs.fed.us, Ecological Process and Function Program

Partners: Oregon State University, Oregon Department of Fish and Wildlife

Thinning and slash treatments dramatically increase deer forage in older even-aged stands in Alaska

TO IMPROVE the management of young-growth stands for multiple values, the station and Tongass National Forest established four operational-scale, widely replicated adaptive management experiments known as the Tongass-Wide Young-Growth Studies (TWYGS). A key goal of TWYGS is to assess the effectiveness of silvicultural treatments for improving forage availability for Sitka black-tailed deer, which is highly valued for sport and subsistence hunting and as prey for wolves and bears. In the fourth TWYGS experiment, thinning and slash treatments were applied to even-aged stands more than 35 years old. Five years after treatment, forage biomass in treated stands was four to six times greater than in untreated stands. Analysis of the biomass data with the FRESH-Deer forage availability model showed that treatments increased deer-days of forage availability by five times in summer and three to four times in winter, depending on the treatment.

Use: Tongass National Forest uses vegetation data in new deer habitat model.

The TWYGS experiments are the primary means for effectiveness monitoring of young-growth management under the Tongass land and resource management plan. The vegetation response data and outputs from the FRESH-Deer forage model are being used by the Tongass National Forest to develop a new deer habitat model for southeast Alaska. This new model will be used for project- and landscape-level planning.

Contact: Michael McClellan, mmcclellan@fs.fed.us, Focused Science Delivery Program

Partner: USDA Forest Service Tongass National Forest

Wolverine habitat projected to decline as climate warms

THE WOLVERINE'S range is confined to cold areas, typically arctic or alpine habitats, where relatively deep snow cover persists through the end of the reproductive denning period in mid-May. In the western contiguous United States, wolverine habitat occurs in an archipelago of alpine meadows and subalpine parklands that contain the climatic conditions necessary for their persistence. In that region, continued warming is expected to cause wolverine habitat to shift upward in elevation, decreasing both its geographic extent and connectivity. Consequently, understanding the potential effects of continued climate warming on the distribution, extent, and connectivity of wolverine habitat is essential for their conservation in the contiguous United States.

Use: U.S. Fish and Wildlife Service uses findings in decision to list wolverine as a candidate species under the ESA.

Researchers modeled the distribution of spring snow cover within the Columbia, Upper Missouri, and Upper Colorado River Basins. They projected that 67 percent of suitable wolverine habitat in the study area will persist through 2030–2059, but only 37 percent will persist through 2070–2099. Although large (>600 square miles) contiguous areas of wolverine habitat are likely to persist throughout the 21st century, such areas will become smaller and more isolated over time. Dispersal modeling indicated that by the late 21st century, habitat isolation will occur at or above levels associated with the genetic isolation of wolverine populations. These findings played a key role in the recent decision by the U.S. Fish and Wildlife Service to list the wolverine in the contiguous United States as a candidate species under the Endangered Species Act.

The lead scientist was interviewed by several media outlets, including National Public Radio and the *Wenatchee World*, *Yakima Herald-Republic*, and *Methow Valley News*, about this wolverine research.

Contact: Keith Aubry, kaubry@fs.fed.us, Ecological Process and Function Program

Partners: University of Washington Climate Impacts Group, USDA Forest Service Rocky Mountain Research Station

About 37 percent of current wolverine habitat is projected to persist through 2099.

Population demography of northern spotted owls analyzes best available science

THE NORTHERN spotted owl, a threatened species under the Endangered Species Act, has become a well-known environmental symbol, and managing for the owl has been a complex issue for land managers. Station scientists collaborated with 27 owl researches associated with 12 institutions or agencies to produce a monograph that provides the most complete picture of the spotted owl's population status to date. It assesses relationships between reproductive and recruitment rates and covariates such as habitat, weather, and the invasive barred owl. *Population Demography of Northern Spotted Owls* demonstrates how collaboration among scientists can provide an analysis template for species assessments and conservation.

The U.S. Fish and Wildlife Service used results from a draft version of this analysis when developing its Spotted Owl Recovery plan. With general release of the book, conservation biologists, federal and state land managers, and the public will have a clear picture of the current population status of northern spotted owls.

Contact: Eric Forsman, *eforsman@fs.fed.us*, Ecological Process and Function Program

Partners: Colorado State University, Green Diamond Resource Company, Hoopa Tribal Forestry, Olympic National Park, Oregon State University, Raedeke Associates, Inc., Simon Fraser University, USDA\APHIS National Wildlife Research Center, USDI Bureau of Land Management, Mount Rainier National Park, USGS Patuxent Wildlife Research Center

For more information: Forsman, E.D.; Anthony, R.G.; Dugger, K.M. [et al.]. 2011. Population demography of northern spotted owls. Studies in Avian Biology No. 40. Berkeley, CA: University of California Press. 103 p.

Northern spotted owl.

Barred owl.

Understanding barred owls habitat preferences may help northern spotted owl recovery

INTERACTIONS with barred owls are a leading cause of the northern spotted owls' continuing decline in the Pacific Northwest. Substantial information on forest structure characteristics used by spotted owls has been collected over the past two decades, but little is known about forest structure characteristics used by barred owls. Understanding barred owls' habitat preferences will help managers evaluate how forest restoration treatments in fire-prone forests may affect interactions between spotted owls and barred owls.

Station scientists used radiotelemetry to conduct the first extensive study of habitat use by barred owls. They learned barred owls use structurally diverse mixed grand fir forest more intensively than open ponderosa pine or even-aged Douglas-fir forest types within their home ranges in central Washington. The scientists shared their findings with the Barred Owl and Modeling Working Groups of the Northern Spotted Owl Recovery Team convened by the U.S. Fish and Wildlife Service. This information has contributed to recovery planning for the northern spotted owl.

Contact: Peter Singleton, *psingleton@fs.fed.us*, Threat Characterization and Management Program

Partners: USDA Forest Service Okanogan-Wenatchee National Forest, U.S. Fish and Wildlife Service

Study identifies causes for demise of sage grouse populations

GREATER sage grouse populations in North America have declined for decades as their habitat has decreased. Station scientists examined how changes in land use could be contributing to these declines. They found that areas where local sage grouse populations had been eradicated had less sagebrush, were at lower elevations, were farther from power lines and communication towers, and were privately owned. Areas of extirpation were more often found along the periphery of the sage grouse range. Rates of habitat decline are increasing across large areas of western sage grouse range from continued and pervasive expansion of invasive plants and associated changes in wildfire regimes. Oil and gas development is also leading to habitat decline.

Use:
Public and private land managers are using results to design and implement sage grouse recovery strategies.

The scientists also measured the threshold values of sagebrush cover and elevation needed by sage grouse. These thresholds values are easily and accurately measured with existing spatial data across the range of the sage grouse.

The U.S. Fish and Wildlife Service used these findings when deciding if listing under the Endangered Species Act was warranted. The agency decided not to list the sage grouse and continues to negotiate changes in landscape management with other federal agencies to prevent future listings. This research provides the scientific foundation for these negotiations. These findings also are being used by private landowners and many different administrative entities that include county, state, and federal planning activities across western North America.

Sage grouse.

Contact: Michael Wisdom, mwisdom@fs.fed.us, Ecological Process and Function Program

Partners: U.S. Geological Survey, Washington Department of Fish and Wildlife

Hope remains for polar bears' sea ice habitat if greenhouse gases are reduced

NO "tipping point" has been reached or is foreseeable for polar bear sea ice habitat over the next century, researchers determined. And, if global greenhouse gas levels are reduced, polar bear populations could be conserved or recovered. This work continues the research that led the U.S. Fish and Wildlife Service (USFWS) to list the polar bear as a threatened species in 2008. It provided

A polar bear near the Beaufort Sea off Alaska's Arctic coast.

new analyses on how several future greenhouse gas scenarios will likely affect polar bear sea ice habitat and populations. The analysis indicates that only major mitigation of greenhouse gasses will avoid sea ice loss and reduce the probability of polar bear populations becoming more vulnerable. It indicates that current sea ice loss resulting from climate change may still be reversible, providing new hope for conserving polar bears. This information can be used by the USFWS to help develop recovery actions for polar bears.

The research appeared as the December 2010 cover story in *Nature*.

Contact: Bruce Marcot, bmarcot@fs.fed.us, Ecological Process and Function Program

Partners: National Center for Atmospheric Research, U.S. Geological Survey, University of Washington

Pacific walrus is vulnerable to continued loss of Arctic sea ice

THE PACIFIC walrus was recommended as a candidate for federal protection under the Endangered Species Act. Before making a final decision, however, the U.S.

Use: U.S. Fish and Wildlife Service uses study as basis for listing walrus as potentially threatened.

Fish and Wildlife Service (USFWS) needed more information on the potential viability of Pacific walrus populations, particularly under climate change and associated human impacts. To help inform that decision, a station scientist projected potential effects of climate change and other stressors on populations of Pacific walrus in the foreseeable future.

The findings were presented to the USFWS, which, as a result, reversed its previous draft finding not to list the Pacific walrus, and instead, listed the species as potentially threatened. This work also provides information on key stressors that could inform the USFWS recovery plan.

Contact: Bruce Marcot, bmarcot@fs.fed.us, Ecological Process and Function Program

Partner: U.S. Geological Survey

Bruce Marcot

Ice floes in the Arctic Ocean north of Alaska. Global warming is causing ice floes to melt sooner in the summer, forcing walrus to haul out on land where they are more vulnerable to predation and have less access to food.

Assessing habitat connectivity, land use, and climate gradients facilitates regional wildlife planning

MANY WILDLIFE species need to be able to move across the landscape in search of food throughout the year. As human populations increase and more land is developed for human

Use: Washington Department of Transportation uses findings in statewide planning.

use, links between wildlife habitats are being lost. To address this, the Western Governors Association Wildlife Corridors Initiative and state wildlife action plans call for incorporating wildlife corridors into regional-scale, long-range landscape management planning.

To help with this process, station scientists worked as part of the Washington Wildlife Habitat Connectivity Working Group to assess regional habitat connectivity patterns for 16 focal species, natural landscape integrity connectivity patterns, and climate gradient patterns. The group completed a geographic information system (GIS) analysis of habitat conditions in the state, which can be incorporated into climate change adaptation connectivity planning. Station scientists provided technical guidance on model development and interpretation and facilitated technical peer review of modeling procedures and reports.

The Washington Department of Transportation is using the information and GIS data produced by the group in statewide transportation planning. The Washington Department of Fish and Wildlife also is using the information in planning efforts, and it is being used to develop decision-support tools under the Western Governors Association Wildlife Corridors Initiative.

Contact: Peter Singleton, psingleton@fs.fed.us, Threat Characterization and Management Program

Partners: Conservation Northwest; The Nature Conservancy; USDA Forest Service Pacific Northwest Region; USDI Bureau of Land Management; University of Washington; Washington Departments of Fish and Wildlife, Natural Resources, and Transportation; Western Transportation Institute

For more information: http://www.waconnected.org/

Learning Events

Forestry professionals learn about recent research on the genetics of host-parasite interactions in forests of western Oregon. Photo by Richard Sniezko.

Symposia, Workshops, and Tours

The Pacific Northwest Research Station sponsors scientific and technical events each year, often in partnership with other agencies, organizations, and universities. Following are descriptions of some of these events.

2011 National FIA User Group Meeting: Twenty-six clients attended this workshop in Sacramento, California. They learned how field measurements are made and used to produce the Forest Inventory and Analysis data used throughout the Nation.

Amphibian Disease Workshop: About 60 people attended this workshop in Gig Harbor, Washington, as part of the annual meeting of the northern regional working group of partners in amphibian and reptile conservation.

American Fisheries Society Symposia: A station scientist played a key role organizing this 4-day annual meeting for more than 5,000 participants. It was held in Seattle, Washington.

BlueSky Training: Station scientists led four training sessions and a webinar for National Forest System staff on using the BlueSky framework to model fire information, fuel loading, smoke dispersal, and more. About 190 people attended the sessions held at different locations throughout the country.

Classrooms for Climate: This symposium, jointly held by the Forest Service and University of Alaska, highlighted research associated with climate change. About 200 people attended the event held at the University of Alaska Anchorage.

Ecological Effects of Invasive Plants: This 1-day meeting of the Western Society of Weed Science included presentations on impacts of invasive, non-native plants on forest, range, grassland, and estuary ecosystems of the western United States, as well as recent advances in research to restore invaded ecosystems. There were 93 attendees.

Elk Habitat Selection in Western Oregon and Washington—Final Models and Management Applications: About 120 people attended this workshop in Portland, Oregon, featuring innovative models of elk nutrition and habitat selection in western Oregon and Washington. The models will benefit current land management plan revisions and habitat management and restoration for elk.

Experimental Forest and Range Network (EFRN) Science Delivery Webinar: The station and the National Council for Air and Stream Improvement, Inc., organized this webinar to learn what would make the nationwide EFRN long-term databases more useful to state and federal water quality regulatory agencies. There were 24 participants.

First International *Ranavirus* Symposium: Twenty-three scientists from nine countries gave presentations that synthesized world knowledge of the pathology, immunology, genetics, and ecology of *Ranavirus*, a virus that is killing amphibians around the world. About 100 participants attended the event held in Minneapolis, Minnesota.

Forest Inventory and Analysis (FIA) Client Meetings and Data Workshops: FIA held a symposium in Anchorage, Alaska, to discuss current research activities in the Pacific Northwest. The following day FIA hosted a data workshop where clients were guided through methods for analyzing FIA data and using them to answer challenging questions about natural resources. About 40 people attended the event. A similar event was held at Magness Tree Farm, Oregon, for 15 members of the Society of American Foresters. A third meeting and workshop was held at Portland State University, Oregon, for about 10 faculty and staff.

Green Peak Study Site Tour: Eight journalism students from the University of Oregon toured the study site as part of a science media project funded by the American Recovery and Reinvestment Act.

Genetics of Host-Parasite Interactions in Forestry: At this 4th international workshop, held in Eugene, Oregon, 87 participants provided overviews of the most current scientific information available on forest insect and disease resistance for a range of forests pests.

H.J. Andrews Experimental Forest: This research site near Blue River, Oregon, hosts many events throughout the year. The annual HJA Day attracted more than 140 visitors. The scientists, students, federal and state land managers, utility managers, and interested public who attended learned about ongoing research in the forest. The Oregon Board of Forestry tour brought together state and federal foresters, private timber managers, and the public to discuss forestry practices. As part of its humanities program, the site hosted seven writers, the Blue River Writers Gathering, and a 2-day long-term ecological research humanities workshop. In total, more than 1,500 people attended events at H.J. Andrews.

Human Influence on Connectivity and Population Structure for River Fishes: A station scientist was the co-coordinator and sponsor for this session of the annual meeting of the 2011 American Fisheries Society. About 50 people attended.

International Association for Landscape Ecology Annual Symposium: The station cosponsored this event with the U.S. chapter of the association, and a station scientist was the program chair. Held in Portland, Oregon, the meeting brought together more than 500 landscape ecologists from the United States and abroad.

Bruce Marcot

Scientists examine maps of study plots on Oregon's Deschutes National Forest.

Introduction to Wildland Fire Decision Support System—Air Quality Tools: A station scientist introduced these tools to about 20 attendees of the Southwest Interagency Fuels Workshop held in Flagstaff, Arizona.

Juneau Icefield Research Program Briefing: Twenty students and faculty from the Juneau Icefield Research Program learned about rain forest ecology, the impact of global warming on glaciers, and the hydrology of glacial streams in southeast Alaska.

Long-Term Ecological Research (LTER) Artist and Science Field Trip: Bonanza Creek Experimental Forest, LTER site near Fairbanks, Alaska, collaborated with 16 local artists to describe the effects of a changing climate on Alaskan boreal forests.

Model Uncertainty: Two half-day workshops engaged extension specialists in discussion of ways to frame the inherent uncertainty and assumptions in the output of most models, and how to discuss that uncertainty in the context of global climate models. Fourteen people attended the workshop in Wenatchee, Washington; 25 attended the workshop in Corvallis, Oregon.

Molalla Forest Productivity Study Field Visits: Six district silviculturists with USDI Bureau of Land Management toured the study site in Molalla, Oregon, to learn about effects of forest harvesting, logging debris manipulation, and vegetation control on Douglas-fir productivity.

North Cascadia Adaptation Partnership Climate Change Fish Workshop: This partnership, organized by station scientists and the University of Washington's Climate Impacts Group, hosted four resource-specific workshops on climate change vulnerability assessment and adaptation planning for the North Cascadia region. About 45 participants from national parks and forests in the region attended.

North Cascadia Adaptation Partnership Project: The station facilitated four climate change education workshops where scientists and resource management representatives presented the basics of climate change science and expected effects on natural resources in the Pacific Northwest. About 340 staff from national parks and forests in the region attended.

Carlos Ramirez

Clients learn about the application of Forest Inventory and Analysis data at a meeting in California.

Smoke and Air Quality Management Tools Training: Station scientists provided training for about 30 attendees at the third Fire Behavior and Fuels Conference of the International Association of Wildland Fire held in Spokane, Washington.

Starkey Experimental Forest and Range Tour: Several tours were held at the experimental forest and range throughout the year highlighting the relevance of past and ongoing research to forest management. About 70 visitors from the Wallowa-Whitman, Umatilla, and Malheur National Forests; Eastern Oregon University; World Forestry Center International Students; and University of Wyoming Cooperating Faculty participated.

Scientists discuss an ongoing study on the Wenatchee National Forest in Washington.

Conservation Education

Pacific Northwest Research Station scientists make time to share their expert knowledge with children, teenagers, and their teachers in a variety of programs ranging from hands-on classroom activities to summer camps.

2011—Year of the Turtle: Station researchers helped organize this worldwide event to raise awareness for turtle conservation, research, and education. For example, activities by fifth graders at Copper Mill Elementary School in Zachary, Louisiana, and by eighth graders at Jane Goodall Environmental Middle School in Salem, Oregon, were featured in a monthly newsletter.

Asa Mercer Middle School Afterschool Program: The station statistician led an afterschool workshop teaching 10 students about scientific inquiry and how to present their project at the Washington state science fair.

BioBlitz: About 30 students from Jane Goodall Elementary and Middle School in Salem, Oregon, learned from station researchers how to conduct a fauna census in and around ponds at the Luckiamute State Natural Area.

Douglas Indian Association Elders and Students Summer Program: Nine participants toured the Forestry Sciences Laboratory in Juneau, Alaska, and learned about job opportunities and research programs. Participants also went on a field trip to the Héen Latinee Experimental Forest, where they learned about natural resource management, hydrology, and the role of the experimental forest in regional studies. They discussed opportunities for Native American students in natural resource management and education.

Ferry Interpreter Training Workshop: Station researchers taught 12 summer interns about rain forest ecology and geology and the natural history of southeast Alaska to prepare them as interpreters.

Forest Camp 2011: Station staff taught 200 sixth-graders about the Web of Life and the importance of fungi in the forest ecosystem. The camp, hosted by the Siuslaw National Forest, was held at Camp Tadmor in Lebanon, Oregon.

Forestry Days: About 300 sixth graders from the Clatsop County school district learned about forest ecology from station staff. The event was done in collaboration with Oregon Department of Forestry.

Becky Bittner

Through the Forest Inside Out! program, 400 children from the Portland metropolitan area learned about nature.

Forests Inside Out! Through American Recovery and Reinvestment Act funding, the station partnered with the nonprofit World Forestry Center in Portland, Oregon, to support a series of 2-day indoor and outdoor experiences for 400 children ages 6 to 10 and family members from diverse and underserved communities in the greater Portland metropolitan area. Eight high school students from the Portland area were hired to act as mentors for the program.

H.J. Andrews Experimental Forest: This research site near Blue Lake, Oregon, hosted field trips and tours for 228 students from elementary, middle, and high schools in the mid-Willamette Valley. The students and their teachers learned about environmental processes and how to conduct research.

I'm Going to College, 2011: A station scientist talked with 60 fifth-grade students about research and opportunities working with the Forest Service. The event was held at the University of Alaska Southeast in Juneau.

Importance of Yellow-Cedar and Its Regeneration to Native People in Alaska: Seven students and elders of the Douglas Indian Association visited the yellow-cedar planting area on Goldbelt Corporation land in Echo Cove, Alaska, to discuss use of yellow-cedar by Native people and learn about forest management efforts to ensure the sustainability of this tree into the future.

Inner City Youth Institute: The station supported the Inner City Youth Institute (ICYI), which encourages underprivileged youth to pursue higher education and careers in natural resource and environmental fields. The ICYI sponsored forest ecology programs in Portland inner city middle and high schools and a summer camp program for high school students from Portland and southwest Washington. This summer's camp was based at Oregon State University, but students explored nearby forests and rivers and visited the Hatfield Marine Science Center on the Oregon coast. The ICYI is a partnership between the USDA Forest Service, Oregon State University's 4-H program, and the USDI Bureau of Land Management. About 200 students participated in ICYI programs.

It All Starts With Plankton: the Marine Food Chain: A station scientist led Earth Day activities for 10 kindergarteners at the Corvallis Montessori School.

Kids in the Creek: This 1-day event provided 200 high school students from Wenatchee School District in Chelan County, Washington, a hands-on opportunity to learn about basic aquatic ecology and conservation.

Knotweed Management Efficacy: Twenty elementary and middle school students in Aberdeen, Washington, learned from a station scientist about controlling an invasive weed during a trip organized by the Chehalis Basin Education Consortium.

Northwest Science Expo: The station sponsored "Outstanding Forest Science" awards to a high school and middle school student at the Northwest Science Expo—a science fair for young scientists, engineers, and mathematicians—at Portland State University.

Oregon Science Teachers' Association: A station scientist gave two lectures on climate change and water to 15 teachers responsible for about 800 students.

Becky Bittner

Children with the Inner City Youth Institute kayak on the Willamette River near Corvallis, Oregon.

Science Workshop for Teachers: The station statistician co-taught a 3-day workshop for the Renton School District through a grant from the Howard Hughes Foundation to the Center for Inquiry Science, Biological Systems Institute. The workshop focused on the process of conducting scientific research and guided teachers through a mini-data collection project.

Terrestrial Amphibians and Road Effects: Station researchers taught 30 students in an eighth grade conservation biology class at Jane Goodall Elementary and Middle School in Salem, Oregon, about this management challenge.

The Investi-gator: Station scientists and their research were highlighted in the climate change edition of this Forest Service publication that is distributed to elementary school children nationally.

Washington State Science and Engineering Fair: The station sponsored an "Outstanding Forest Science Project Award" at the Washington State Science and Engineering Fair at Olympic College in Bremerton, Washington.

Honors and Awards

Photo by Pete Bisson.

2010 Regional Forester's Partnership Award

John Lundquist, a forest entomologist in the Threat Characterization and Management Program, was honored for his outstanding contributions in engaging youth, families, and communities in outdoor experiences and natural resource stewardship through the Youth Employment in Parks Program.

2011 Environmental Excellence Award

Peter Singleton, an ecologist with the Threat Characterization and Management Program, received this award from the Federal Highway Administration for his exemplary achievement in Ecosystems, Habitat, and Wildlife for the Washington Connected Landscapes Project: Statewide Analysis. The assessment will influence many aspects of construction and maintenance of Washington's highway system.

2011 National Wilderness Award

Don McKenzie, a research ecologist with the Threat Characterization and Management Program, received this award for his research exploring the challenges of adapting to changing disturbance regimes while maintaining the integrity of wilderness areas in a warming world.

David F. Thomas Award

Paul Hennon, a research plant pathologist with the Threat Characterization and Management Program, received this national award from the Forest Service for his outstanding customer service as a forest health expert.

Excellence in Science

Dede Olson, a research ecologist with the Land and Watershed Management Program, was honored by the Society for Northwestern Vertebrate Biology for her service to the society as both its president and vice-president.

Excellence in Science and Technology

Michael Furniss, a hydrologist with the Communications and Applications Group, was honored by the Chief of the U.S. Forest Service for his efforts to communicate science and build tools that enable the application of science to pressing land management problems.

Exemplary Case Study

The Integrated Landscape Assessment Project, led by **Miles Hemstrom** with the Focused Science Delivery Program, won recognition as one of eight "exemplary case studies" by the Farm Foundation, and was selected for presentation at the Agriculture, Food, Nutrition, and Natural Resources Research and Development roundtable in Washington, DC.

Fulbright Scholarship

Michael Wisdom, a research wildlife biologist with the Ecological Process and Function Program, taught and conducted ungulate research at the Aridlands Research Institute in Mendoza, Argentina. Recipients of Fulbright grants are selected on the basis of academic or professional achievement, as well as demonstrated leadership potential in their fields.

Highly Cited Authors

Marty Vavra, Catherine Parks, and **Michael Wisdom,** with the Ecological Process and Function Program, received the Highly Cited Author Award 2007–2010 from the journal *Forest Ecology and Management.* Their paper, "Biodiversity, Exotic Plants, and Herbivory: the Good, the Bad, and the Ungulate" (2007), was one of the journal's top 50 cited papers.

Olaus J. Murie Award

Michael Wisdom, a research wildlife biologist with the Ecological Process and Function Program, was honored by the Rocky Mountain Elk Foundation for his work on the science of wildlife management. The award is based on five criteria: (1) relevance of work to the conservation of wild, free-ranging elk; (2) application of work "on the ground" to benefit wild, free-ranging elk; (3) dedication to his profession; (4) commitment to the conservation of wild, free-ranging elk; and (5) credibility and respect among peers.

Outstanding Achievement Award

Paul Hennon, a research plant pathologist with the Threat Characterization and Management Program, was recognized by the 2010 Western International Forest Disease Work Conference as the individual who has contributed the most to the field of forest pathology in western North America.

Research Spotlight

Steve Wondzell, a research ecologist with the Land and Watershed Management Program, was a contributing author of the article "Zooming in on aquatic denitrification hot spots," which was featured as a Research Spotlight in EOS, the American Geophysical Union's weekly publication of transactions.

USDA Honor Award

Charlie Crisafulli, an ecologist with Land and Watershed Management Program, was honored for his personal and professional excellence in communicating the significance of long-term research at the Mount St. Helens National Volcanic Monument to the scientific community, policymakers, and the public.

USDA Secretary's Award

Brad St. Clair and **Randy Johnson,** research geneticists with the Land and Watershed Management Program, were recognized for their work with the Conifer Translational Genomics Network Coordinated Agricultural Project.

PNW Research Station Organization

Station Director
Bov B. Eav
P.O. Box 3890
Portland, OR 97208-3890
Phone: 503-808-2100
E-mail: beav@fs.fed.us

Assistant Director
for Administration
Lesley A. Kelly
P.O. Box 3890
Portland, OR 97208-3890
Phone: 503-808-2102
E-mail: lakelly@fs.fed.us

Assistant Director for
Communications and
Applications
Cynthia L. Miner
P.O. Box 3890
Portland, OR 97208-3890
Phone: 503-808-2135
E-mail: clminer@fs.fed.us

Assistant Director for
Program Development
Paul Brewster
Forestry Sciences Laboratory
11305 Glacier Highway
Juneau, AK 99801-8545
Phone: 907-586-7801
E-mail: pbrewster@fs.fed.us

Assistant Director for Research
Susan A. Willits
P.O. Box 3890
Portland, OR 97208-3890
Phone: 503-808-2115
E-mail: swillits@fs.fed.us

Program Managers

Ecological Process and Function
Beatrice Van Horne
Forestry Sciences Laboratory
3200 SW Jefferson Way
Corvallis, OR 97331
Phone: 541-750-7357
E-mail: bvhorne@fs.fed.us

Focused Science Delivery
R. James Barbour
Forestry Sciences Laboratory
P.O. Box 3890
Portland, OR 97208-3890
Phone: 503-808-2542
E-mail: jbarbour01@fs.fed.us

Goods, Services, and Values
R. James Barbour (Acting)
Forestry Sciences Laboratory
P.O. Box 3890
Portland, OR 97208-3890
Phone: 503-808-2542
E-mail: jbarbour01@fs.fed.us

Land and Watershed Management
John A. Laurence
Forestry Sciences Laboratory
P.O. Box 3890
Portland, OR 97208-3890
Phone: 503-808-2191
E-mail: jalaurence@fs.fed.us

Resource Monitoring
and Assessment
Gretchen Nicholas (Acting)
Forestry Sciences Laboratory
P.O. Box 3890
Portland, OR 97208-3890
Phone: 503-808-2034
E-mail: gnicholas@fs.fed.us

Threat Characterization
and Management
Marcia Patton-Mallory
Forestry Sciences Laboratory
1133 N Western Ave.
Wenatchee, WA 98801
Phone: 509-664-1715
E-mail: mpattonmallory@fs.fed.us

Western Wildland Environmental
Threat Assessment Center
Nancy Grulke
3160 NE 3rd Street
Prineville, OR 97754
Phone: 541-416-6583
E-mail: ngrulke@fs.fed.us